Now more than ever, business and policy leaders need to harness and realize the unparalleled power of capitalism. This book shows us how.

—MAGGIE WILDEROTTER
Former Chairman and CEO,
Frontier Communications

Neither an encomium nor a dirge, but a thoughtful, practical analysis of how business leaders can help repair the weaknesses in American capitalism and make it perform better for all of us.

—ALICE M. RIVLIN
Senior Fellow, The Brookings Institution
Founding Director, Congressional Budget Office

No method of organizing economic activity has done more for the prosperity of the ordinary person than capitalism. It has harnessed the desire to deploy capital and one's intellect and labor to do better for one's family by meeting the needs of others. However, course corrections are periodically required to make it work fairly for everyone. *Sustaining Capitalism* offers the perfect course correction for capitalism—one that gives every citizen a shot at realizing the American Dream.

—RON WILLIAMS
Former Chairman and CEO, Aetna

This thought-provoking book provides a bipartisan roadmap to how business leaders and policymakers can make capitalism work for all— to ensure that every citizen gets a shot at realizing the American Dream.

—ROGER W. FERGUSON, JR.
President and CEO, TIAA

Americans are rightly worried about prospects for long-term growth, but a deeper concern is declining trust in public institutions—can government work for growth—and do so for everyone? All business readers should read this book—a manifesto of the need to stand up for free enterprise and for policies that help it raise living standards. *Sustaining Capitalism* offers bipartisan solutions in key policy areas and in reforms to make government more accountable. This book offers a call to action to business leaders to reclaim their role in the public square.

—GLENN HUBBARD
Dean and Russell L. Carson Professor of Finance and Economics, Columbia Business School

While one might debate any specific policy proposal in this thoughtful book, the authors make an important call to business leaders to engage more deeply in the public square to help bridge today's partisan divide.

—GEORGE BARRETT
Chairman and CEO, Cardinal Health

Sustainable solutions to America's toughest challenges will require bipartisan support, and this book presents a range of common sense ideas to grow the economy, secure our fiscal future and move the country beyond political gridlock.

—MICHAEL A. PETERSON
President and CEO, Peter G. Peterson Foundation

SUSTAINING CAPITALISM

Bipartisan Solutions to Restore Trust and Prosperity

Steve Odland

Joseph J. Minarik

Committee for Economic Development
a division of The Conference Board, Inc.

1530 Wilson Blvd, Suite 400, Arlington, VA 22209

The Conference Board, Inc.
845 Third Avenue, New York, NY 10022

Production Management: Michael Bass Associates

This book is printed on acid-free paper.
Manufactured in the United States of America

ISBN 978-0-692-76970-6 (Hardcover)
ISBN 978-0-692-81958-6 (Paperback)
ISBN 978-0-692-82006-3 (Kindle)

First Edition
22   21   20   19   18   10   9   8   7   6   5

CONTENTS

ABOUT CED

The Committee for Economic Development of The Conference Board (CED) is a nonprofit, nonpartisan, business-led public policy organization that delivers well-researched analysis and reasoned solutions to our nation's most critical issues.

Since its inception in 1942, CED has addressed national priorities to promote sustained economic growth and development to benefit all Americans. CED's work in those first few years led to great policy accomplishments, including the Marshall Plan, the economic development program that helped rebuild Europe and maintain the peace, and the Bretton Woods Agreement that established the new global financial system, and both the World Bank and International Monetary Fund.

Today, CED continues to play an important role through its trusted research and advocacy. Comprised of leading business executives, CED lends its voice and expertise on pressing policy issues. In recent decades, CED has made significant contributions across a broad portfolio, including pre-K education importance and funding, bipartisan campaign reform, corporate governance reform, U.S. fiscal health, academic standards in K-12 education, post-secondary education access and achievement, importance of STEM education, immigration, free trade, foreign assistance, women on corporate boards, Medicare and broader health care reform, crony capitalism, inequality, judicial selection reform, child care, the role of business in promoting educational attainment, digital learning, teacher compensation and quality, corporate short-termism, federal tax reform, social security, innovation and growth, reducing global poverty, welfare reform, and more.

CED's work is based on seven core principles: sustainable capitalism, long-term economic growth, efficient fiscal and regulatory policy, competitive and open markets, a globally competitive workforce, equal economic opportunity, and nonpartisanship in the nation's interest. CED's research findings are disseminated widely, achieving tangible impact at the local, state, and national levels.

www.ced.org

ACKNOWLEDGMENTS

This book is truly the work of all of the dedicated members and staff of the Committee for Economic Development of The Conference Board (CED).

CED was founded in 1942 by business leaders who sought to advance the nation's interest through nonpartisan public-policy research. Their selfless efforts helped to give the United States and the world the Marshall Plan, the Bretton Woods monetary agreement, the Employment Act of 1946, and confidence in their collective economic future. Walking in their footsteps, today's CED Members sought in this book both to commemorate the 75th anniversary of the CED and to map the way to a new confident future through their own public-policy insights, rooted in their business experience and expertise. We thank them for their dedication to developing reasoned solutions in the nation's interest.

We thank especially Joseph E. Kasputys, a long-time CED Member and former co-chair of the CED board, who contributed generously with his passion, time, insights, and financial support to make this project possible.

A small group of CED Members, including Michael G. Archbold, Paul Atkins, Bernard C. Bailey, W. Bowman Cutter, Patrick Gross, Hollis Hart, Bruce K. MacLaury, and Lenny Mendonca, devoted considerable time reading the manuscript and providing insight.

We'd like to recognize Monica Herk and Diane Lim, who contributed to CED policy statements that underlie some chapters in this book. Courtney Baird and Alison Snyder provided research assistance. Joseph DiBlasi managed the logistics of the book. Other CED staff members, including Mike Petro, Mindy Berry, Cindy Cisneros, Caroline DeLancey, Sean Hicks, and Amanda Turner, supported the production of this book.

Anthony J. Corrado, Jr. of Colby College directed past CED projects on campaign finance and judicial selection reform on which portions of this book were based. Thomas Kiely, Lori Cavanaugh, Matt Rees, Peter Drubin, and Kathleen Mercandetti provided editorial and graphical assistance. Michael Bass took the book through the final production process. Mark Fortier provided promotional guidance.

This project also was made possible in part by generous support from the Ford Foundation, to finance the gathering of working groups of outside experts to critique selected segments of the book.

At the end of the day the authors accept all responsibility for any errors of commission or omission.

— Steve Odland and Joseph J. Minarik

The Challenge and Opportunity of Sustaining Capitalism

THE UNITED STATES historically has been and continues to be the most prosperous nation in the world. It is the leader in geopolitics and the standard-setter in virtually every aspect of modern life worldwide. This "land of opportunity" has been a haven for innovators and tinkerers—where poor children could become steel magnates and college dropouts could create global technology powerhouses, where "creative destruction" provided opportunity for both individual workers and their companies to reinvent themselves time and again. Yet, in this traditional home of pioneering spirit and entrepreneurial passion, the fundamental economic system that unleashed this unprecedented prosperity is under question and even under attack.

Millions of Americans are seeing their incomes stagnate or decline. They are losing faith in the American dream of upward mobility and in

American-style capitalism itself. Trust in established businesses, banks, and more broadly in the institutions of government is at historic lows. Too many of the latest generation of Americans to enter the workforce, the "millennials," see an economy that seems to fail their parents or themselves. Thus, they see no reason to support that economic system. More than half of Americans between the ages of 18 and 29 say they do not support capitalism.[1] Other surveys suggest that those millennials have come to prefer socialism, perhaps using a very broad interpretation of the term, or lacking experience with its history of failure in practice.

Unfortunately, for our economy as a whole, failure breeds failure. Risk-taking and initiative, the building blocks of economic growth and prosperity, require confidence. Potential innovators who see weak businesses and hesitant consumers hold back, which hinders growth and progress. Thus, such stagnation is self-reinforcing.

Although the torpid economy is troubling, the loss of societal trust is perhaps most painful. For decades, Americans generally believed that their public institutions, including government, would ultimately do the "right thing" in the broadest terms.[2] At the very least, even when people disagreed with their fellow citizens, they accepted that those with whom they disagreed had the nation's best interest at heart. Now, the public dialog has coarsened and questioning the motives and loyalties of political opponents is routine. Our political rules and institutions, which are predicated on maintaining the status quo (absent some measure of bipartisan consensus to take action), are gridlocked on many of the most urgent public issues.

Historically, a key contributor to the success of U.S. capitalism has been its remarkable public support (which has been nurtured, of course, by robust economic performance). The erosion of public support today is thus a matter of considerable concern. Business leaders have a responsibility as well as a self-interest in showing the way toward harmonizing individual interests with the common good. To date, business's voice and example have been generally characterized as ineffectual. *New York Times* columnist David Brooks has written, "Business leaders have been inept when writers, intellectuals and politicians attacked capitalism."[3]

Business must do more to help restore U.S. prosperity, which will require difficult choices and leadership. Business leaders must make their case for the free-enterprise system, and for its contribution to the nation's standard of living as well as its standard of transparency and accountability. And they must engage in the public debate—both as listeners and as contributors of their experience and expertise—about policies and reforms to restore economic growth and trust in our national community.

■ ■ ■

In the wake of the financial disruptions of the last decade, most notably here in the United States but also in many other developed and developing free-enterprise economies, the most basic optimistic assumptions and attitudes about growth and prosperity have eroded. Today's economy and society are reminiscent of the United States in the 1930s when fear begat fear, and the economy remained stagnant until the onset of World War II shocked it to life. People talked then of a "crisis of capitalism," and believed that the booming wartime economy could fall right back into the Great Depression when the war ended.

And that is where we, the Committee for Economic Development (CED), enter this story. This book takes its inspiration from CED's founding in 1942, when a small circle of U.S. business leaders gathered to identify solutions that would restore order to a global economy. Similarly, it was in response to a more recent crisis in American capitalism, following the financial downturn of 2008, that CED launched a multi-year research project on *sustainable capitalism*.[4] This book, designed for business leaders and policymakers, is the culmination of those research efforts. Its publication appropriately coincides with the 75th anniversary of CED.

We at CED see an urgent need for revisions in both business practices and public policy if our economic system is to reestablish consistent economic growth and regain the trust of the American public. We write this book as our contribution toward resuming respectful dialog among what have become disparate and distrustful public factions. And we hope to convince our fellow business leaders that we need to engage the entire business community in public dialog and dedication to private best business practices. In the chapters that follow, we remind our readers of why the free-enterprise system has earned—and deserves—its reputation as the preeminent form of economic organization, respond to what we believe are inaccurate accusations toward that system, and focus on remedies to legitimate concerns.

The analyses and recommendations presented in this book, aligned with other activities the CED is undertaking in connection with its 75th anniversary, underscore our fervent belief in the free-market economic system—our nation's brand of capitalism, which has brought wealth and higher living standards to the United States and countries throughout the world. We see no more important task than to pursue CED's ideals: long-term economic growth; efficient fiscal and regulatory policy; competitive and open markets; a globally competitive workforce; equal economic opportunity; and nonpartisanship in the nation's interest. In short, we seek to make American capitalism sustainable, and to unite Americans of differing persuasions behind the core principle that the U.S. free-market economic system can be made to work for all of us.

HISTORY

First, what is this capitalist economic system that we seek to sustain? To answer that, we must begin by addressing an even more basic question: What *is* an "economic system"? One answer comes from the writings of Adam Smith, who is identified by many as the eighteenth-century founder of modern economics. Although he did not create or establish the economic system of his time and place—what we now call "capitalism"—he observed, described, and analyzed what he saw already happening around him, with people acting in an instinctive and un-self-conscious way. Smith recognized that the "invisible hand" delivers optimal outcomes because people—given the institutions of personal freedom and protection of private property—quite naturally choose how to work, save, and invest in ways they believe are best and most valuable. Thus, economists would say, markets drive efficient use of resources.

Prior to Adam Smith, there were alternative "economic systems," which were generally based on sovereign fiat. The crown might command the allocation of labor, and people would be put in roles that suited the crown's wishes rather than those that generated the most value. The crown might allocate investment resources to projects that were gratifying to the crown rather than value-creating. In fact, it was probably some knowledge of such mistaken choices of command economies that caused Adam Smith to recognize as remarkable the achievements of the un-self-conscious free-market or "capitalist" economy, and inspired him to write *The Wealth of Nations*.

Following Adam Smith, other thinkers proposed more consciously designed alternative economic systems, such as socialism and communism. Today, most U.S. economists would characterize those systems as versions of "resource allocation by the sovereign" even if the objective guiding this new sovereign was ostensibly a more egalitarian distribution of resources. Those alternative economic systems proved to be less successful than free-market capitalism; indeed, almost all have disappeared. While some former communist powers continue to pursue "state-owned" or "state-directed" capitalism, few economists expect those economies to do better, over time, than the command economies they replaced. What progress they have made owes much to the free-market reforms that they have finally put in place. Still, those economies make up in quantity (of population, in China, and of some natural resources, in Russia) for what they lack in the quality of their resource allocation, and so they remain a factor in the global economy. In some European capitalist systems, government plays a far greater resource-allocation and regulatory role than it does in the United States, though still far short of the degree of government control over the economy we see today in China.

The Value of Free Enterprise

Wherever it has been practiced, capitalism has raised living standards and reduced poverty on an epic scale. But its value runs even deeper. Compared with a command economy, capitalism requires that individuals are free to allocate their spending and savings where they perceive value, to offer their labor where they perceive the greatest reward, and to form businesses if they so choose. By allowing the full use of all human resources, capitalism has achieved enormous economic progress, along with opportunity for individuals. These elements of personal freedom are so basic that they are often forgotten, or at least underappreciated, by many who decry our capitalist system.

These elements of personal freedom are also components of democracy. People who can say "no" to orders about where they should work, or what they may or may not do with their money, clearly have rights. From those rights flow the rights to vote, speak, and attempt to influence civil society. Thus the foundations of capitalism are closely aligned with the foundations of democracy, personal freedom, and equality of opportunity.

While capitalism has made America the most prosperous nation in history, that prosperity is not solely a byproduct of capitalism. Where capitalism has been allowed to function elsewhere around the world, it has raised living standards and reduced poverty, but other capitalist nations have not had the full U.S. measure of success. Other attributes of the United States—including its location out of the reach of potential enemies and its natural resource endowments—clearly contributed. Also clearly contributing was another family of attributes as well: the character of our people. Perhaps because the settlers of America from the early part of the modern era were self-selected people willing to risk and strive to achieve a better life, and because those settlers have been followed by succeeding generations through the same self-selection, the American people have been uniquely successful in achieving that better life. Even Americans who did not come here freely have joined in building and adhering to a moral-cultural system, built on civic institutions, which has guided U.S. business leaders to what John Fletcher Moulton termed "obedience to the unenforceable," or adherence to a set of values—such as initiative, hard work, self-reliance, personal integrity, and stewardship— that established standards of propriety and behavior.

The future of the U.S. global economic leadership depends upon the willingness and ability to maintain those American ideals, including fundamental principles of equality and personal freedoms and rights that flow from our democratic capitalist economic system. These principles are essential not only because they maintain our national spirit from within but also because they give us firm footing when we seek to establish standards of behavior in geostrategic terms as well as in international trade and finance. Thus, to sustain prosperity, we must rededicate ourselves both to the open-market competition that undergirds capitalism, and to the principles of freedom, equal rights, and ultimately democracy that flow from the workings of capitalism.

Recent Crisis

With all due acknowledgement to the theoretical and historical merits of U.S. capitalism, how has the capitalist system performed in recent years, especially during and since the financial crisis? The capitalist world has been rocked by the greatest economic and financial crisis since the Great Depression. In fact, the outcome could have been far worse than it was. Fortunately, crisis management and policymaking, though not perfect, were better this time around than in the 1930s. Nevertheless, economic performance has been below-trend since the financial crisis. Historically, deep recessions have been followed by steep economic recoveries, but—per the warnings of economic historians who have studied past financial crises—this recovery has been disappointing.[5] Aggregate economic growth is slower than the post-World War II average.[6] This "Great Recession" is surely a wake-up call for the keepers of our economic system.

But was this colossal downturn with only a sluggish recovery the result of some inherent flaw in capitalism, such that free-market nations should search for some fundamentally different alternative? In our judgment, the answer is no. Capitalism cannot and does not eliminate either poor judgment or malfeasance. It can only provide incentives for better performance over the long run. Government must establish rules to ensure fair play by all.

In the period leading to the financial crisis, many economic players—some with considerable responsibility and presumed financial sophistication—clearly failed to recognize that U.S. real estate was in a bubble.

It's also clear that some other actors within the financial sector took advantage of people of lesser sophistication. No one should accept such failings, particularly given that they had such extraordinarily damaging consequences.

There always are humans of differing ethical values, who will take advantage of others in both command economies and under capitalism. Corruption in several of the former communist countries continues to far exceed that in our economic system, largely because communism and other state-controlled systems concentrate authority and hence the impact of poor judgment or malfeasance. Demonizing all of business because of the financial crisis is clearly wrong. For example, many non-financial firms—along with their employees and shareholders— were among the victims. In a market economy, we do need rules and their enforcement to deter and prevent such destructive behavior.

Nevertheless, even in good times, some economic players fail to adjust to or simply miscalculate market changes or competitive threats, and as a result businesses fail and employees and investors are hurt. The market itself punishes such poor judgment. These are the risks of the market; without the risk of money being lost, money cannot be made.

An alternative economic system that bestows universal wisdom and can perfect human nature has not yet been found. The best path forward for the United States, in our view, is to enforce fair rules and common ethics, pursue equality of opportunity, and mitigate the shocks of rapid economic change, not to search for some fundamentally different economic system that promises to prevent economic and market volatility.

Still, the substandard U.S. economic performance, in both the financial crisis itself and the recovery from it, has left many Americans disillusioned and demoralized. They include a population of idle and underemployed workers with a strong perception that the game is rigged—that they are under-rewarded for their efforts (or their willingness to exert effort), while they view others either to be grossly over-rewarded or even to have profited from malfeasance. Many of these disaffected persons would say that the reason for their economic suffering is the failure or malfunctioning of the U.S. capitalist system. Others believe that government policy failures of overregulation, overtaxation, and overspending are responsible for sub-par economic performance.

Some economists argue that the weakness in wages, employment, and economic output is caused by transient, cyclical factors. Others argue that the arrival of the long-delayed full and robust economic recovery will right the balance between the earnings of rank-and-file workers and the salaries and bonuses of investors and players on Wall Street. But at some level, it does not matter. Sophisticated analytics aside, consumer and citizen morale has declined, and so the tone of both civic and economic life has soured, perhaps to the point of long-term damage. Consumer demand, labor supply, worker commitment, and civic engagement all suffer. Whatever the cause and whether particular critics are right or wrong, a significant share of the population is not keeping up—and feels it can't—with what's needed to prosper in today's economy. That is an urgent problem.

Meeting the Challenge

As members of the broad business community, we find the current public disquiet over lagging growth in living standards and consequent inequality a serious concern and a call to action. The strength of the U.S. economy, as well as public confidence in the country's economic institutions, rest on a principle that always has been fundamental to the success of American capitalism: the interdependence of the interests of society and business. The U.S. economy has prospered as corporations grew and invested, thereby creating jobs, innovating products and services, generating value and opportunities for suppliers and product users, boosting living standards in the communities in which they operate, and paying taxes. For decades U.S. corporations have provided their employees with health insurance and retirement plans—benefits that are provided by government in many other countries.

By the same token, corporations prosper when society supports the economic conditions that foster competition and growth. On balance, Americans uniquely have been receptive to the "business of business" for two centuries. Conditions that foster a healthy business environment include an effective and equitable legal system, clear and efficient regulation, sound fiscal policies, modern infrastructure, and a healthy financial system. These contribute to wealth creation in capitalist economies. Social investments in the education of citizens and the general workforce, and in infrastructure and public goods (such as national defense and research), also strengthen the potential for businesses and societies to prosper.

This interdependence of interests has created a virtuous cycle that has generated U.S. prosperity. But that virtuous interdependence is under pressure today, threatening the long-term sustainability of our nation's economic system that has generated such unprecedented prosperity. This threat of fissure impels this book.

Since its inception in 1942, the CED has advocated policies to achieve long-term economic growth that benefits all Americans. A consistent theme throughout the CED's 75 years of work has been that economic success for all is an outcome of the healthy interdependence of business and society.[7] Business leaders in their own interest must drive changes that advantage both business and society. To renew and restore that cooperative interdependence today, to re-achieve the long-term dynamism and vitality of the U.S. economy, the business community faces a two-fold challenge. First, business leaders must change their own business practices to demonstrate that constructive interdependence with society. And second, they must take the risk to re-enter the public square to make the case for sound public policymaking aimed at the future prosperity of all of the American people.

The first challenge requires a fundamental change in managerial focus. Old conceptual frameworks that pit owners against other stakeholders in a zero-sum struggle over competing goals are outdated and self-defeating. Increasing numbers of executives have adopted a new framework that recognizes the interdependent role of multiple stakeholders—customers, employees, owners, creditors, suppliers, communities, and the environment—in creating long-term value.

Corporations today are under intense pressure to balance and meet the expectations of these multiple constituencies, and public trust in business leadership only modestly has improved since the worst of the financial crisis. Customer dissatisfaction over product or service quality, discord between employees and management, public protest over offshoring and wage deflation of middle-income jobs, and acrimony between communities and businesses seeking to expand operations have been growing, fueling public distrust. Ultimately, the long-term value of companies and even the viability of the U.S. economic system are threatened by the persistence of outdated frameworks that set corporations and their stakeholders at odds.

Apart from shareholders and other traditional economic interests, stakeholders including nonprofits or non-governmental organizations (NGOs) increasingly are making social demands on how private businesses raise standards for labor conditions, environmental management among their suppliers, and human rights issues. Of course, there are limits to what each corporation can afford to do on its own to meet the (sometimes conflicting) interests of multiple constituents. Some executives fairly ask, where is the line between private and public responsibilities?

There is a fairly natural link between the multi-stakeholder perspective and taking a long-term view of business value creation. Firms that practice "quarterly capitalism" and focus on short-term returns to shareholders will be more likely to forgo investments in additional production capacity, employee training, or research and development so that they can "hit their numbers." In contrast, a business that aims to create enduring value more likely will be there for its stakeholders for years to come. But what accepted standards of behavior can guide executives when quarterly profits alone are no longer an acceptable measure? We discuss the pursuit of long-term value through a multi-stakeholder perspective in Chapter 3.

Outside of the firm's gates, business must contribute its experience and insights in the national debate over the direction of public policy. Policymakers must strengthen the societal conditions for prosperity, and business leaders have important wisdom to bring to the table.

The nation is falling behind international competition in several key respects, and so policymakers must act on multiple fronts.

- Fundamental to every other public issue, our policymaking apparatus is rusted and erratic, both failing to act and acting in counterproductive ways. Even worse, the public has become dangerously cynical and is convinced that the economic game is rigged with "crony capitalism." Such manipulation also favors incumbent businesses over innovators, slowing job creation and economic growth. We recommend important reforms to improve the public-policy process and, equally important, regain the public trust.

- The health of public finances is in free-fall. Our national debt burden—the size of our public debt relative to the size of our economy, out of which that debt must be serviced—is growing unsustainably. The unresolved crisis in public finances is just one example of why the constructive interdependence of business and society must be rebuilt. A nation lacking public consensus will have even more difficulty achieving the painful compromises that are essential for the good of the whole. We use business skills to analyze the problem and identify feasible solutions.

- Central to that public debt problem, and important to the stagnation of household incomes and the drain of business investment resources, is the rising cost of health care. Our health care system, for all of its miracles in delivering heroic remedies, is inefficient and delivers poor value for money overall. We propose ways to make quality care and universal access compatible with affordable costs.

- Today's young Americans are falling short of youth in our competitor nations in both knowledge at any particular educational level, and attainment of college degrees. Today's workers are not keeping up with skill needs, and are tripping over transitions from obsolete to cutting-edge jobs. This is a trajectory toward decline and decay, and education is central to creating equality of opportunity and therefore social mobility. We document the existence of the problem, and recommend solutions extending from early childhood through workforce development.

- Our regulatory system is generating questionable new rules and ignoring the failings of old ones. Inefficient regulation can be a roadblock to job creation and growth of economic output and incomes. We provide some lessons from the latest scholarship on the issue and from improved and superior practices around the world, and discuss how to balance the need for access to credit with the safety of financial institutions.

- Finally, the United States must redefine its role in a changing world economy. As technology topples barriers to international commerce, the counterproductive instinct to protect the past can obscure the need to compete for the future. We explain why business, like individuals, must accept the need to stand up to international competition.

For some years now, business leaders have shied away from the public square, after playing a leading and constructive role in the national policy debate for many years. It is time for the business community to re-engage as true economic patriots. The stakes have become much too high to remain silent.

We do not believe that a good outcome of any public debate over the merits of capitalism would be a victory for one side and a silencing of the other. Rather, the best outcome would be a meeting of the minds: an economy, a nation, and a society in which all sides can work through their differences and agree on measures that will deliver greater growth and opportunity for people throughout the United States and around the world.

Capitalism requires competition, which inevitably has relative winners and losers. But the U.S. economic system should continue to provide equal opportunity and reward effort. It should yield market-based, widely accepted outcomes. This will foster greater equality and greater prosperity—not because those outcomes are forced, but because the capabilities and opportunities are greater for everyone in our society. We are all in this together. We want this book to contribute to a vigorous—and hopefully in the end a unifying—public debate that will make capitalism sustainable.

1

The Structural Threats to Capitalism— And the Structure of a Solution

AMERICAN CAPITALISM is at a crossroads: decline or renewal. Structural forces are at work that can either enervate or energize the nation's economic engine of prosperity, built on its capitalist foundation. The outcome will depend on how U.S. business and policy leaders shape these forces, and through them, capitalism's future.

We are not alone in recognizing a deterioration of the quality and tone of American life. We believe that, at its root, this is because millions of Americans are not participating in America's economic expansion. As a result, many Americans see a discouraging future, devoid of the traditional optimistic American dream of upward mobility. Trust in all manner of institutions, including business, banks, and government—but reaching even further—is at historic lows. That loss of trust extends to our economic system itself. The millennial generation, in particular, expresses its disillusionment with American-style capitalism, and a growing interest in socialism as an alternative, according to troubling public opinion polls.

Polls or surveys are snapshots that can capture moods and attitudes. They are subject to error and are quickly reversible. Polls, in other words, can mislead. Many young Americans surely associate "capitalism" with the financial crisis of the last decade, which everyone acknowledges as a serious failure. And many young Americans likely do not know what strictly defined "socialism" is; they would be unlikely to support government ownership of the means of production, including the businesses for which they work.

Still, public trust in the institutions of our political economy is undeniably eroding. If this trend continues, it could become a threat to capitalism itself: no economic system is sustainable if a significant number of its participants lose faith in it. A disillusioned and frustrated public could support political overreactions that could cause irreversible damage to our economic and policymaking systems.

So, constructive change is needed urgently. But because our political system was designed to favor stability over change, the current polarized political environment could also prevent the very reforms that are so urgently needed. We need an understanding of our economic ailments and a functional political system based on public trust.

THE PROBLEM

Why are so many Americans disillusioned about our nation's economy, its basic fairness, and their place in it? Why do they believe that our leaders and institutions have ignored their concerns? The single word that captures their mood is "unfairness." Americans across the political spectrum consistently tell pollsters that the growing gap in wealth and income troubles them. Over the past 40 years, economic inequality (by any measure) has been increasing. After the transformative events of World War II, the U.S. economy enjoyed more than two decades of extraordinary growth and a general narrowing of inequality. But then this broad-based progress stalled, and that is the basis, we believe, of much of today's distress and unrest. (See Figure 1.1, "Total Market Income Shares of the Top 10 Percent of U.S. Households.")

FIGURE 1.1   Total Market Income Shares of the Top 10 Percent of U.S. Households (percent)

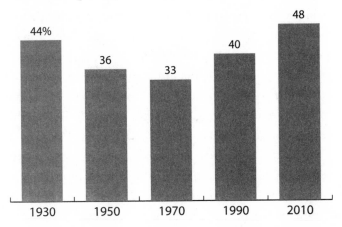

Source: Facundo Alvaredo, Tony Atkinson, Thomas Piketty, and Emmanuel Saez, "The Database," World Top Incomes Database, 2015. (http://topincomes.parisschoolofeconomics.eu/#Database:)

Our economy always has exhibited some measure of inequality. That is not surprising. Individuals differ in their skills, aptitudes, and willingness to take risks. And those who take risks to innovate and invest can, if successful, generate the jobs and incomes that the American people need, and can earn substantial incomes. But other risk takers meet with less success—for themselves, their investors, and their employees (who often invest through stock options and pension plans). Thus, an economic system that allows market forces to reward success will have some measure of inequality. Trying to enforce equal outcomes can stifle that innovation and growth.

Over the last several decades, however, inequality in the United States (by any measure) has been increasing markedly. Since the early 1970s growth has generally been slower, and inequality has generally grown. This has been true of all measures of economic well-being: market incomes, after-tax after-transfer incomes, and wealth.[8] Some analyses suggest that the current degree of inequality is at or near its level just prior to the Great Depression in 1930, the highest in modern times.

Some, but not all, of the increasing inequality of the last four decades has resulted from spectacular returns to highly successful innovations and investments. In fact, although the public debate has focused on the metaphorical "1 percent" and many data sources—including the one we use here—do not provide additional detail, rising inequality has been driven mostly by outsized gains in income and wealth far higher in the population, perhaps the highest 0.1% or even 0.01% of households.[9] Some of these outsized gains are understandable. The highly success- ful enterprises of recent years *by definition* provided substantial value to a large number of people, who became their customers and generated those returns. And many of the individuals who profited so spectacularly were line employees with stock options, not executive decision makers.

But some of the rising inequality has reflected lagging real income growth for a large segment of the working American population (see Figure 1.2). We find that exceedingly troubling. CED always has cham- pioned economic opportunity broadly and fully shared. This is the essence of the American dream.

Furthermore, there's concern that inequality is increasing to poten- tially unhealthy levels. A broader and deeper base of consumer demand can lead to steadier and more reliable growth. A more even distribution of income and wealth driven by greater equality of opportunity provides the most benefits for the broader population. As one reflection of this line of thought, a Standard & Poor's report of August 1, 2014, concluded that income inequality stifles U.S. growth.[10]

But inequality also can degrade the tone of American life. While soci- eties differ in the extent to which social mobility is possible, the prom- ise of the "American Dream" long has been that anyone, including the poorest of the poor, can rise to the top by dint of hard work—and that children can reach a better life than their parents. This belief is deeply ingrained in the national psyche, and its realization has been a part of the American experience. For example, the probability that a child whose parents are in the bottom fifth of the income distribution reaches the top fifth has been estimated at 8.4 percent for children born in 1971, and 9.0 percent for children born in 1986. For those in the second lowest

FIGURE 1.2   Cumulative Growth in Average Inflation-Adjusted Market Income, by Market Income Group, 1979–2013

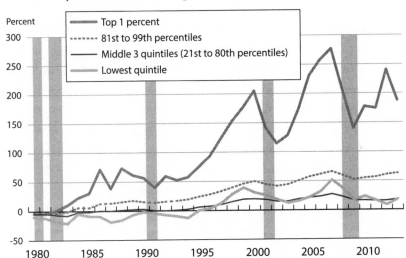

Source: Congressional Budget Office, *The Distribution of Household Income and Federal Taxes, 2013*, June 2016, figure 8, page 15. Available online at: https://www.cbo.gov/sites/default/files/114th-congress-2015-2016/reports/51361-HouseholdIncomeFedTaxes.pdf.

Market income consists of labor income, business income, capital gains (profits realized from the sale of assets), capital income excluding capital gains, income received in retirement for past services, and other sources of income. Government transfers are cash payments and in-kind benefits from social insurance and other government assistance programs. Those transfers include payments and benefits from federal, state, and local governments.

Income is converted to 2013 dollars using the personal consumption expenditures price index.

Income groups are created by ranking households by market income, adjusted for household size. Quintiles (fifths) contain equal numbers of people; percentiles (hundredths) contain equal numbers of people as well.

quintile, the chances of rising to the top were 17.7 percent and 13.8 percent, respectively. Thus a child has about a one in ten chance of truly "making it," and the likelihood has been rising slightly. (Note that this statistic reflects annual income rather than wealth.)[11]

A somewhat different research finding is that social mobility in the United States has stayed more or less constant over the last 50 years.[12] But consider that if income outcomes were merely a random draw, then the chance of any child reaching the top 20 percent of the income distribution would be 20 percent. What's more, social mobility in the United

States is actually lower than in most Western European countries that have a similar per-capita GDP.

Excessive inequality and reduced social mobility can be mutually reinforcing. For instance, education is key to successful social mobility, and children from the highest-income families have a higher probability of undertaking advanced education, even relative to lower-income children with superior secondary school achievement.[13] Career opportunities are also key to mobility, yet even as more career opportunities for women and minorities have opened up during that last couple of decades, social mobility has not grown appreciably.[14] So rising U.S. inequality also reflects what may be a damaging decline in equality of opportunity—and without opportunity, the American Dream becomes a nightmare.

THREE STRUCTURAL FORCES, AND THEIR CONSEQUENCES

Why have U.S. economic performance, and most importantly broad-based income growth, fallen so far behind our experience and our expectations? Fundamental to this basic economic trend is the recent slowdown in U.S. productivity growth, which drives our current discontent over slow wage growth, makes the coming fiscal challenges more daunting, and aggravates many more of our national problems. But U.S. output per worker has stagnated since the financial crisis, while output per hour has turned negative (see Figure 1.3, "U.S. Productivity Growth"). Businesses have been adding workers, but output has still lagged. Aggregate hourly compensation for U.S. workers has finally come out of its stall, but without productivity growth, the staying power of wage growth is uncertain.

Economists don't agree on the sources of the productivity slowdown. Taxes, government spending, debt, and regulation are the smoking gun for some observers. For others, it's sluggish new business growth, labor market skill deficiencies, tepid investment, a paucity of game-changing innovations, or the slow pace of efficiency improvements. Still others speculate that the sheer ferocity and enormous disruption and demoralization of

FIGURE 1.3   U.S. Productivity Growth

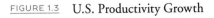

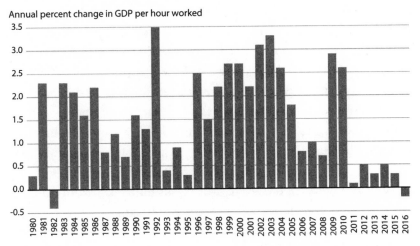

Source: The Conference Board. https://www.conference-board.org/data/economydatabase/index
.cfm?id=27762

the downturn have made recovery a very long road to hike. Demand is weak. GDP growth is anemic. The stagnation in overall productivity, which is stifling economic growth, has also coincided with the slowdown in wage growth, and the increase in economic inequality.

But there is some agreement about three fundamental forces that lurk behind the painful wage slowdown and rise in inequality: the technology revolution, the globalization of our nation's economy, and the fast growth in scale and scope of the financial sector.

Technology. Technological innovation improves lives and generates enormous wealth and economic leadership for America. It is at the root of all of the improvement in U.S. living standards in the past, and it will be the essential ingredient in restoring the nation's confidence in our free-market system and expanding opportunity in the future. However, in the short run, technological innovation also can worsen inequality and disrupt lives unless America's leaders act to offset the "destructive" side of this "creative destruction."

Technology continues to advance at a rapid pace, auguring still more change to come. By one estimate, of the 5 million jobs lost during the eight years preceding the financial crisis and its downturn, four out of five were automated, not shipped overseas.[15] Some scholars have concluded that most jobs that can be "offshored" ultimately will be automated.[16] Artificial intelligence and advanced robotics technologies are beginning to be used by companies to automate specific work tasks (individual activities, that is, rather than whole jobs)—including tasks conducted by high-wage employees. These technologies could dramatically change how businesses organize work in the generation to come. As many as 45 percent of specific work tasks humans perform today— activities that represent nearly $2 trillion in annual wages—could be automated, according to some analysts.[17] The pace of technology-enabled business model disruption—think of Apple's incursion into music distribution, Amazon in retail, Uber and Lyft in the transport sector, and Airbnb in hospitality—may even be accelerating. It might seem convenient to regulate new technology to protect existing jobs. But such "crony capitalism" would stall U.S. economic growth. Technological advances that we forgo will become barriers as they are adopted in other nations with which we try to compete in the future. How can the United States remain the world's industrial and commercial leader after we voluntarily cede our technological edge? Consumers have benefited greatly from technological advances. Although technology may have caused some job dislocation, it has created even more new jobs. The creation of new and innovative businesses, not the protection of old, incumbent businesses, is the key to future job growth.

It might seem illogical to speak about the role of technology in transforming work, and at the same time to bemoan slow productivity growth. In fact, the illogical coexistence of the two may suggest that our economy has been thrown off track by the financial crisis and its aftermath, and that with the resumption of more vigorous demand growth and investor optimism, technological advances may begin to drive more rapid productivity growth. In any event, there is little doubt that the financial crisis has disrupted our financial system and put a damper on the "animal spirits" that provide an intangible force behind the pace of economic growth.

Globalization. Global trade can subtract some jobs from the economy, but at the same time it can add higher paying ones while lowering the cost of goods consumers and businesses buy. The ultimate problems are not byproducts of increased global trade, the rise of cross-border production networks and the growth of overseas production, and the de-layering of old industrial integrated value chains into subsectors of specialist suppliers. Those are advances driven by the free-market system, which will be adopted all around the world. If the United States fails to do so, they will be used by foreign competitors to capture U.S. jobs anyway.

The immediate effects of globalization and technology are very similar. The deployment of robots on manufacturing floors and of automated check-in kiosks at airports (reducing labor), the relocation of people in call centers, and the substitution of automation for them are all part of an inevitable, logical progression of the efficient re-allocation of resources that characterizes capitalism and why it works. As technology and globalization transform industrial sectors and work, they also change the balance of value for skills. A generation ago, the vast majority of prime age men—those between the ages of 25 and 54—participated in the workforce, whether they had a college education or not.[18] But by 2015, participation had declined, and only 83 percent of non-college–educated prime age men participated in the work force, according to a recent study by White House Council of Economic Advisers.[19] By contrast, 94 percent of such men with college degrees had jobs. More than one-third of prime age men outside the workforce live in poverty. Declining demand for skills that are vulnerable to outsourcing and technology is part of the problem, the study suggests. Other studies have chronicled the growing wage gap (over more than 30 years) between those with a college degree and those without.[20]

In this respect, these adverse effects of globalization and technology are very similar. They are byproducts of how leaders in business, education, and government manage (or fail to manage) the social impact of the inevitable and irreversible forces of the market, including job displacement, skill obsolescence, and wage suppression that accompany these trends. Lacking have been thoughtful, balanced programs to address the inevitable fallouts from this process. Whether trade and technology can be made to contribute to broadly shared prosperity depends on whether Americans can embrace the upside and ensure against the downside through public policies and sound private decision-making. If trade and technological change are managed creatively, employees and communities impacted when production is automated or moves overseas can seize new opportunities in other industries (including exporting) and make the economy grow.

Finance. No modern economy can be successful without a strong financial sector. New and expanding businesses need capital to maintain economic growth and rising living standards. The U.S. financial sector is uniquely effective in aggregating capital, and then allocating that capital to productive investment opportunities. It has introduced innovative products to boost market liquidity and hedge risk, and to provide the fuel that keeps the whole market economy running and transacting smoothly. Such innovation is vital to supply financing everywhere it is needed in the economy, and especially to help modest-income households to build home equity and form new businesses, so that they can begin to realize the American dream. For U.S. capitalism to be sustainable and to make our economy competitive in today's world markets, we need a vibrant financial sector.

But risky loans and new, complex financial instruments also contributed to the economic crash and caused enormous harm to many families and institutions. The financial sector also created some of the most enormous incomes and fortunes that inflated inequality, but sometimes in fashions that did not generate real value for rank-and-file consumers; in that respect, inequality caused by rising incomes at the very top of the scale was not productive, and possibly harmful.[21] How America chooses to reform finance will determine whether the sector achieves a better balance of vitality and stability, or an imbalance toward either calcification or instability.

More broadly, the market economy can tend to produce relatively high, even super-normal, returns to capital, particularly financial capital, compared to labor. Why? The financial sector grew enormously over the decades running up to the financial crisis, arm-in-arm with economic growth and globalization. A broad survey[22] calculates that in 2006, value added in the U.S. financial sector, much more narrowly defined than the finance, insurance, and real estate (FIRE) sector, peaked at 8.3 percent of GDP, versus 4.9 percent in 1980, and just 2.8 percent in 1950. (There are contrary views, however, using different measures. The finance employment share has been declining since 2003, and in 2014 stood at just 4.3 percent of all nonfarm employment, a lower share than any of the output share measures.[23]) But to the extent that finance has grown, higher-income households who tend to hold relatively more capital and depend relatively less on their income from working than do lower-income households have benefited disproportionately. Growth in the return to capital (relative to labor) reinforces and accentuates differences of income and wealth across the social spectrum, widening the gap between the rich and poor.[24]

The fundamental forces of technology, globalization, and growing financialization are creating an increasingly knowledge-based U.S. economy that favors the highly skilled and well educated. Flexible labor markets that reward valuable skills, innovative disruption of business models, and the efficiencies that come from automation all contribute to keeping capitalism healthy. But keeping capitalism healthy also means paying attention to the social impact of the disruptions inherent in these forces. Capitalism must evolve to continue to create value for all—through vision and policy tools that complement and enhance the workings of the market, rather than trying to restrict or control it.

THE ROLE OF PUBLIC POLICY: INVESTMENT IN EQUALITY OF OPPORTUNITY

To continue to lead the world, the U.S. economy and its capitalist system need reforms to education, government, regulatory and tax systems, and businesses practices that will create value for all stakeholders. The United States needs to invest in its future. Although the three key forces of technology, globalization, and finance bring enormous growth and competitiveness to the U.S. economy, they simultaneously collide with, and change the face of, the nation's economic landscape. The resulting problems must be met just as the opportunities must be pursued. The United States cannot allow the downside of economic evolution to eclipse the upside—rather, we must ensure that capitalism remains a healthy, positive force for prosperity.

Globalization, technology, and the growth of the financial sector aren't the only drivers of inequality, and economists will always differ on the causes. But those forces unquestionably have contributed to job losses, wage suppression of low-skill workers, wage inflation for high-skill workers, and economic deterioration of many American communities, particularly smaller, rural ones.

Whatever the drivers may be, inequality can be reduced and social mobility can be improved—and the pain of globalization and automation somewhat assuaged—if the United States were to more thoughtfully and systematically invest in the prerequisites for *equality of opportunity* to flourish. This means reforming education, increasing and widening employee skills development, and providing economic transition assistance for affected families and communities. It means rebuilding trust in the economic system, including combating any disproportionate influence that incumbent, entrenched special interests can have on policy at the expense of the creation of new, innovative businesses and new jobs. It means making a fractious Washington work once again, so that the policy reforms needed to make capitalism sustainable for all don't die in gridlock. It also means mending the United States' fiscal ill health, so that resources can be matched to the economic priorities of public investment in infrastructure, research, and education. And it means re-thinking trade policies to free global trade in the achievement of domestic production and growth.

Creating the conditions for equality of opportunity to flourish, however, does *not* mean enforcing *equality of outcomes*. Dictating incomes does not increase production; it does not increase the nation's standard of living. Over the long term, trying to remedy inequality or stalled wage growth solely through tax- and command-based redistribution schemes will impair the economy and stifle innovation. Seeking equality of outcomes through redistribution does not address the real problem, which is the absence of true equality of opportunity and resulting wage growth. Ultimately, it makes everyone poorer. Giving every worker the skills and the chance to live up to his or her full potential would both raise the bottom and the middle, and advance the nation as a whole.

THE ROLE OF BUSINESS

America's business leaders understand that their companies' interests are integral to the strength and vibrancy of the nation and of society— of customers, employees, owners, suppliers, business partners, creditors, communities, and the public. Business enterprises do not stand apart from the system that supports them. Many business leaders also understand that the interconnection of a business and the system that supports it brings unique responsibilities. They understand the need to act as stewards, not only of their own companies but also of the society in which their organizations operate. CEOs need to focus on their companies—and boards of directors and shareholders must ensure, through oversight, that they do.

But the long-term success of the company may require making repairs to the society in which it operates. And given the stress in our society today, an executive's focus must expand to meet this challenge.

The health of our society and domestic economy needs business leadership in the public square as well. The nation must regain civility in public discourse and find common ground to make sound public policy. Business leaders and CEOs in particular credibly can speak to issues that most directly affect the long-term contribution of their companies to the society at large, including the soundness of the markets they serve, the availability of well-trained workers, and the strength of the economic and social environment.

To be clear, this does not mean that CEOs, in their capacity as business leaders, should become partisans of purely social and political issues. As private citizens, of course, they should express themselves as they individually see fit. But as business leaders, they can—must—use their public positions to take stands in critical public policy decisions that affect the long-term viability of capitalism, and therefore the health of our society. They must pound the table in defense of capitalism. It is time for business leaders to stand up and lead.

THE STRUCTURE OF A SOLUTION

So we see structural economic forces—technological change; globalization; and counterproductive financial engineering—as key players in the interrelated problems of inequality; slow income growth; widespread popular disillusionment, cynicism, and distrust of what were not so long ago bedrock American institutions; and a coarsening and polarization of our national life and dialog. In the face of these challenges, society today teeters between gridlock and destructive overreaction on key issues that need constructive action.

Against this background we offer a structure for thinking about solutions. That structure builds upon both public policy reforms to provide the prerequisites of renewed income growth through a sound economy, and best business practices to establish transparency and fairness. Those public-policy and business reforms, when firmly established in reality and in public perception, can support renewed public trust and confidence in our nation, its economy, and our public institutions. And as members of the business community, we see an essential business role in both public-policy and business-practice reforms—speaking out in the public square while maintaining our own house—to earn the public trust and confidence that will rest upon them.

2

Crony Capitalism

SINCE THE FOUNDING of the United States, widespread public support for capitalism has nourished the remarkable success of the U.S. economy. But that support has been eroding in recent years, for three inter-related reasons. First, there's been a steep decline in public support for the economic system and its major institutions—business and banks in particular—because of the poor performance of the economy since the 2008 downturn.[25] Second, most Americans are deeply disturbed by the uneven distribution of economic gains that's been exacerbated by globalism, technology, and winner-take-all (and to some, "owner-take-all") employment dynamics.[26] Third, the majority of Americans, from across the political spectrum, have come to view public policy decisions as primarily reflecting the interests of the rich and well connected.[27] We discuss the first two reasons elsewhere in this book; the third of these is the topic of this chapter.

Public-private collusiveness isn't unique to the United States, of course, and it pervades the economies of many other nations far more than it does here.[28] Yet, the game is rigged, say a significant number of Americans, who believe economic outcomes are pre-determined to favor the few who already are ahead. Along the entire political spectrum—from far left to far right—there is growing belief that the economic success some enjoy arises from close relationships between private interests (such as businesses, nonprofit institutions, and labor unions) and their lobbyists on the one hand, and government on the other.

To the extent that real, or even perceived, unfair private advantage fuels growing disillusionment of the American public, public-private coziness poses a serious long-term threat to the success of America's brand of capitalism.

Reducing the extent to which private interests influence public policy for their own gain won't solve all that contributes to American disillusionment. But it would help re-instill a sense of fairness in the economic system, reduce public suspicion, and restore trust in our system.

There is another important reason to throttle back private influence over government. Coziness impairs the economy. Many of the favored-treatment deals that are eroding public support in the economy— cash subsidies, tax preferences, earmarked appropriations and no-bid contracts, regulatory and trade protections—inhibit the productive allocation of society's resources and reduce innovation and economic growth. They tend to play to the advantage of incumbent interests instead of new businesses, stifling innovation. In the long term, if innovations are not achieved in the United States, our competitive advantage will erode.

Crony behaviors harm both the economy and society over the long run, and businesses and business organizations engaged in what amounts to a game of insider rent-seeking should be focusing their energies on more productive pursuits, such as innovation and job creation. So cronyism must be addressed if capitalism is to be sustained and strengthened. Remedies for reducing cronyism largely lie in policy reforms. But business leaders must play a role in helping to set the terms of the debate about cronyism and standards of behavior. They should use their positions to inform the public and policymakers of its dangers.

UNHEALTHY RELATIONS BETWEEN BUSINESS AND GOVERNMENT

"Crony capitalism" is the term the public has adopted for the seeming pervasiveness of these deals. We use the term advisedly and uncomfortably.

Crony capitalism has become a rallying cry for some who indict the entire business community, and capitalism itself, as corrupt. That is not our intent here. But public concern ought to be addressed openly and thoughtfully, and the problems and challenges of crony capitalism must be debated nationally. Using the public's own terminology for this phenomenon is probably the only place to start.

The incidence of cronyism has risen in tandem with the growth of government as an economic actor. The stakes for influencing policy to unfair advantage are greater, as are the opportunities to achieve influence—particularly with the growing dependence of politicians on money and lobbyists.

Interactions between business and government are necessary, and in fact, business and government are interdependent. Their cooperation can and should benefit the overall U.S. economy over the long run. The market yields the best outcomes, but when market imperfections arise, public policy must intervene if the economy is to attain—or sometimes just to approach—optimal outcomes. When government intervenes effectively, good public-private "deals" follow. For instance, markets yield efficient outcomes if there are many producers, so that none has absolute market power; but if there is only one producer, or merely too few to make a competitive market, the seller can restrict supply and extract excess profits from consumers. The formation of a monopoly is one kind of "market failure." Government can restore competition (which inevitably is easier said than done) by restricting monopolies.[29]

But the very concept of a market failure is controversial. Because perfectly competitive markets are extremely rare, we judge real-world markets based on relative degrees of imperfection, not by clear and absolute standards. One person's perceived monopoly, for example, is another person's hard-earned success in a competitive market. Such judgments are sometimes cut along clear partisan lines. For instance, some might assess monopoly power in our economy through the lens of labor bargaining power rather than through industry structure.

This underscores the challenge of defining precisely what constitutes "crony capitalism." Just as market failure is to a considerable degree in the eye of the beholder, so too the incidence of "crony capitalism." Because market failure can require government intervention in the economy, "crony capitalism" cannot be defined as *any and every* government intervention. Rather, crony capitalism would constitute government intervention *not* justified by market failure, but instead as part of a pursuit of a *narrow, purely personal, or organizational* interest through some subsidy (whether delivered through public spending or as a tax preference) or some regulatory protection against fair competition.

In other words, not all public-private deals are an inefficient allocation of the nation's resources. A government intervention that effectively addresses a market failure may not benefit every interest in society, but should benefit society *as a whole.* Some crony deals might be zero-sum transactions—for example, a dispute over which interest gets to use an economic resource (perhaps which bidder gets a concession to operate a restaurant location on a limited-access public highway), where the economic consequences would be identical whichever bidder wins. However, a truly bad crony deal might prevent an innovator from challenging an incumbent business with a new and superior technology. In that instance, deprived of additional competition and innovation, society as a whole suffers—even though the protected interest may benefit. If an incumbent interest can protect an inferior product, service, or process merely to safeguard its own advantaged position, we have cronyism at its worst.

Unhealthy government interventions are made on behalf of many interests, including business, labor, the tort bar, nonprofits, lobbyists, and particular subgroups of the population. The merit of a deal, not its source, defines cronyism. For business, crony deals can take many forms, including the following ones catalogued by researchers at George Mason University's Mercatus Center:[30]

- Obtaining exemptions from legislation or securing the passage of legislation to provide targeted benefits;
- Effecting regulatory changes, exemptions from regulation, or regulations that discourage new or small competitors;

- Obtaining targeted tax breaks or modification of tax penalties;
- Securing direct or indirect subsidies;
- Obtaining tariff or quota protection from foreign competition;
- Gaining access to bailout funds or loan guarantees; and
- Securing benefits from non-competitive bidding.

To better understand the distortionary effect of crony activity, consider a few well-known examples.

- The U.S. government protects the domestic sugar industry by shielding producers against foreign competitors through import tariffs and quotas. It also shields the industry against low prices through a non-recourse loan program that serves as an effective price floor. Sugar producers argue that current policy keeps prices of the commodity stable, thereby avoiding the issuance of subsidy payments characteristic of other sectors of agriculture. The price for this subsidy: U.S. consumers and businesses that use sugar as an input have had to pay twice the world price of sugar on average since 1982. Recent estimates put the annual direct cost to consumers at almost $4 billion per year.

- Taxpayers additionally cover the cost of subsidized loans to sugar producers, through payments to foreign producers as compensation for import quotas below levels set in trade agreements, and potentially through subsidized sales of excess sugar to motor-fuel producers for use in ethanol production. Sugar-using companies, such as producers of finished food products, have opposed these subsidies without success. Those firms are estimated to have lost about 20,000 jobs because of the higher cost of sugar.[31] Most of the benefits of protection have accrued to a handful of sugar-producing corporations, which have engaged actively in lobbying and in financing political campaigns. This sector spends disproportionately higher amounts on lobbying than all other American crop sectors.

- The Export-Import (Ex-Im) Bank's mission is to provide financing guarantees for U.S. exporters to risky overseas markets. Defenders of the bank argue that all of our major competitor nations have such export-financing facilities, and that Ex-Im is needed to level the play-ing field. Further, they argue, if we hope to negotiate away such facil-ities in future trade talks but eliminate our own facility now, this equivalent of "unilateral disarmament" would allow our competitors to refuse to yield in negotiation and to retain a significant compet-itive advantage. Critics of the bank charge that it is an explicit sub-sidy to its selected beneficiaries. They note that the Ex-Im instead has leaned toward safe deals in safe markets often for large businesses that the private sector would be more likely to finance.[32] The lineup of U.S. firms on the two sides of this debate is indicative of the differ-ence of point of view. U.S. aircraft manufacturers, for instance, sup-port Ex-Im to help them to sell in other markets, while U.S. airlines oppose it on the ground that it allows cheaper acquisition of U.S. air-craft by their overseas competitors.

- In the energy sector, the United States provides subsidies to both the fossil fuel and renewable energy subsectors. This is emblematic of the contradictions underpinning long-term U.S. energy policy and speaks to how politics can infect policy.

- Antitrust exemptions for unions, and particularly the ability of pub-lic-sector unions to collect mandatory dues and then contribute to the political campaigns of the officeholders who will negotiate their pay and benefits, are questionable public-private deals in the eyes of many. Critics also point to the Davis-Bacon Act (which supports wage lev-els in public projects), and the Jones Act (which restricts shipping between U.S. ports to U.S. constructed and flagged vessels using U.S. labor) as examples of crony labor union deals. The Jones Act, for instance, has had a particularly perverse effect of increasing costs and inhibiting commerce.[33]

There are many more examples. In the defense industry, allegedly, contractors have spread manufacturing and construction work across the country so that if a program is challenged the largest possible number of members of Congress will find their constituencies adversely affected.

(Others contend that such diversification of suppliers increases national security by making the supply chain less vulnerable to disruption.)

Similarly, the federal government undertakes numerous projects that many see as having essentially local rather than national benefits, such as water and beach restoration projects, or transportation or other infrastructure projects. Influential legislators arguably use their power to secure local benefits at the expense of the federal Treasury. Medicare's system of administered prices creates the opportunity for favoritism and manipulation. Tax expenditures—amounting to "spending through the tax system," as some critics charge—cost the Treasury hundreds of billions of dollars a year.[34] The exclusion from measured income of employer-paid health-insurance premiums is one such preferential provision of the tax system. Retirement savings tax deductions, and deductions of state and local tax paid, are other examples of preferential measures that arguably provide the most benefits to taxpayers with the highest incomes.

THE CAUSES AND TOOLS OF CRONY CAPITALISM

Over the past few decades, government has become an increasingly important player in the U.S. economy. Total U.S. federal and local government spending was 17.2 percent of GDP in 1948, and under 25 percent of GDP as late as 1957, but peaked at 37.0 percent of GDP in the wake of the financial crisis in 2009, and remains at 31.8 percent at the end of fiscal year 2015.[35] This growth has given the government substantially increased influence over the allocation and use of resources in the economy.

The large relative increase in public spending has been accompanied by an explosion in government regulation, which not only channels government spending but also controls and constrains private-sector behavior in non-governmental activities. Each year from 1997 to 2006 there were around 80 new "significant" regulations (defined as those costing around $100 million each).[36] Beginning in 2007, there was a sharp increase in the pace of regulation, reaching 150 significant new regulations a year by 2011. Whereas in 1950 there were fewer than 20,000 pages of federal regulations, today there are in excess of 165,000 pages. By the regulatory agencies' own estimates, the total cost of complying with their rules could easily exceed $100 billion, with each year's new rules adding more than $10 billion to the total.[37]

This growth in government involvement in the economy has provided elected and unelected officials with greater opportunities to influence economic outcomes in favor of those who can most effectively petition the government. Like yin to yang, this has led to a rapid increase in spending by special interests to influence regulation and policy more generally. Private interests use two primary tools to influence government: campaign financing and lobbying.

Campaign financing. Since the mid-1990s, the cost of U.S. political campaigns has skyrocketed. Whereas in 2000 the total cost of the presidential and congressional campaigns was a little over $3 billion, by 2012 the total cost had increased to nearly $7 billion. By 2012, the estimated average cost of winning an election to the House of Representatives had increased to $1.5 million while the average cost of a successful Senate race had increased to almost $9 million.[38] Figures for the 2016 election cycle—funds raised and spent—almost certainly will exceed the 2012 number.

Political scientists have advanced several plausible reasons as to why U.S. elections costs have escalated, from the realities of modern campaigning—with professional pollsters, consultants, television advertising, and social media targeting—to the need for candidates and their parties to campaign continuously. Independent spending also fuels rising election costs. These are expenditures intended to advance the cause of a particular candidate for election but undertaken by an outside entity, nominally without coordination with the candidate's own campaign. From 1992 through 2012, independent expenditures increased by a factor of 100, from $10.9 million in 1992, to $143.6 million in 2008, to $1.0 billion in 2012. Corporations and labor unions were allowed to make independent expenditures in 2012 as a result of the Supreme Court's 2010 decision in *Citizens United v. the Federal Election Commission*. While the fear was that these newly empowered entities (especially large corporations) would spend heavily, this has not happened. Instead, wealthy individuals and labor unions have been the primary source of this substantial increase in independent spending.[39]

Whatever the reason for the escalation in election campaign costs, political candidates have become highly dependent on private sources of funding to secure re-election, and raise campaign funds—continually. By one estimate, most congressional incumbents spend between one-quarter and one-third of their time in campaign fundraising activities. This creates pressure to conform their views and their voting patterns to the wishes of major campaign donors. It may mean that candidates who are more willing to accept the requests of donors are more likely to win election. It has also contributed to at least a public perception of politicians "owned" by large donors who ask for favors—the embodiment of "crony capitalism."

Lobbying. The third largest sector in Washington, after government and tourism, is lobbying, an industry that has mushroomed since the late 1970s. There were 11,518 full-time professional lobbyists registered by Congress in 2015, representing virtually every type of interest in America, according to the Center for Representative Politics (CRP). Estimates of the total number of persons employed in Washington who either are lobbyists or are associated with them surpass 100,000. The CRP estimates that over the past 15 years the amount of money spent on lobbying has more than doubled to reach its present level of around $3.2 billion. But that does not include money spent for grassroots organizing, coalition building, issue advertising, or for advocacy on the Internet, to communicate with policymakers indirectly. (None of these fit the legal definition of lobbying.) Some estimate that total spending to influence public policy in Washington is close to four times the officially reported amount.

The Constitution protects the right of citizens to petition their government, and lobbying can fulfill a legitimate need of lawmakers and public administrators for information and perspective about the workings of the private sector. Lobbying can inform elected policymakers about what the private sector needs to increase incomes and create jobs. But lobbying can be abused. Economist Luigi Zingales has observed that industries in which the government has become an important regulator or protector are particularly liable, in view of their close contact with the government, to seek more extensive government aid.[40] Lobbyists for business interests also seek to reduce government influence on their clients' activities, or to pursue intervention that tilts the playing field in their favor. In some circumstances, influencing government regulation—to forestall competition from innovators who threaten to unseat incumbent interests, for instance—can be a more profitable use of business funds than cutting costs or developing new products.[41]

Corporations and trade associations account for around 85 percent of what is spent on lobbying federal and state-level government. In addition, large organized interest groups and groups that are supported by large corporations are much more likely to lobby on their own behalf than smaller groups.[42] The returns from targeted lobbying can be very high, which creates an incentive for still more lobbying.[43] For example, a Sunlight Foundation analysis of 200 corporations found that between 2007 and 2010 companies investing heavily in lobbying paid significantly lower effective federal tax rates than those that did not.[44] According to the study, six of the eight companies that invested the most in lobbying between 2007 and 2009 saw effective-tax-rate declines of at least seven percentage points—in contrast to the median tax rate decline among all 200 companies of 0.6 percentage points.[45] A number of lobbying firms advertise that $1 invested in lobbying can yield as much as $100 in benefits.

Coinciding with the growth of lobbying has been increased recruitment of well-placed policymakers into lobbying as a second career. Prior to 1973, about three percent of former congressmen or senators took up employment as lobbyists upon leaving office. Today, around 40 percent of former congressmen and 50 percent of former senators are lobbyists. The same is true of former senior House and Senate staffers. It is also reported that an increasing number of former (and perhaps also future) lobbyists are to be found in senior congressional staff positions, and senior positions in the Executive Branch, subject to some restraints.

In a much-cited study, researchers Richard Hall and Alan Deardorff found that lobbyists tend to concentrate their efforts on politicians who are already most convinced of their positions. Hall and Deardorff argued that lobbying was in effect a matching grant of costly policy information, political intelligence, and labor to strategically selected legislators.[46] A Harvard University law professor, Lawrence Lessig, considers the intersection of lobbying, campaign finance, and economically invasive government to be a fundamental part of a "gift economy."[47] Although there might be no formal quid pro quo between congressmen and lobbyists, congressmen are under increasing pressure to bend their views to satisfy lobbyists who choose to offer ongoing support and help in raising campaign finance. Several well-respected politicians, including John McCain and Chuck Hagel, have described lobbying in less flattering terms. In their words, the confluence of U.S. campaign finance and lobbying has effectively become a system of legalized bribery.

The nexus between lobbying and campaign contributions can flow both ways. Lobbyists (and other private-sector officials) are frequently approached by elected policymakers and asked to deliver campaign finance with a clear subtext that their interests will be adversely affected otherwise.[48]

THE ECONOMIC COST OF CRONY CAPITALISM

More than two centuries ago, Adam Smith emphasized how costly crony capitalism can be, and economists have added to the economic case against cronyism ever since. Cronyism imposes a tax on the public by distorting the proper functioning of the market economy for the benefit of a select few.

"People of the same trade seldom meet together, even for merriment and diversion, but the conversation ends in a conspiracy against the public, or in some contrivance to raise prices," Smith observed in *The Wealth of Nations*. "It is impossible indeed to prevent such meetings, by any law which either could be executed, or would be consistent with liberty and justice. But though the law cannot hinder people of the same trade from sometimes assembling together, it ought to do nothing to facilitate such assemblies; much less to render them necessary."[49]

In the 1980s, an American economist, Mancur Olson, argued that the comparatively greater economic return gained by private interests through lobbying, versus through increased production, is more than just a perverse incentive for businesses to invest in politics rather than innovation. It "influences the attitudes and culture that evolve in society," Olson said. "Lobbying increases the complexity of regulation and the scope of government by creating special provisions and exceptions. A lobby that wins a tax reduction for income of a certain source or type makes the tax code longer and more complicated; a lobby that gets a tariff increase for the producers of a particular commodity makes trade regulation more complex than if there were a uniform tariff on all imports and more complex than it would be if there would be no tariff at all."[50]

Although the costs of crony capitalism on the U.S. economy intrinsically are difficult to measure (because they embrace and involve virtually every sector of not only the domestic economy but virtually every economy overseas that competes with ours) they are substantial. Crony capitalism reduces the overall degree of competitiveness of the U.S. economy. It does so by impeding new entrants and innovations through tax exemptions or spending or low-cost credit for established firms, or through a complex regulatory environment. Those measures favor incumbents at the expense of new entrants and innovators, and contribute to increased market concentration.[51] This slows economic growth and job creation, and gives more nimble economies overseas an advantage over domestic firms.

One reflection of crony capitalism in the United States has been the substantial increase in industrial concentration over the past six decades. This concentration has been detrimental to both competition and innovation. In the financial sector, big banks have become behemoths while the small banks have disappeared or shrunk. In the non-financial sector too, economic activity has moved away from small and medium-sized enterprises to large corporations.[52]

Crony capitalism also reduces the drive for innovation and for minimizing costs and maximizing consumer benefits. Why invest to compete when the returns on blocking competition can be higher? A study of cronyism, looking at 8,000 companies in 40 developing nations, concluded that the advantages of influence could lower costs associated with regulation, increase pricing power, and increase access to credit. But compared to companies with less crony influence, crony-dealing companies tended to invest less in R&D, introduce fewer new products, and achieve lower productivity.[53]

Rent-seeking through subsidies or tax benefits for vested interests at the expense of others distorts the natural re-allocation of resources in the economy. Subsidies for corn production, for instance, have led to large increases in the prices that the U.S. public pays for gasoline, corn, and many food products.

Finally, crony activity impedes fundamental economic reforms that could yield substantial efficiency and equity gains to the economy and for which there might be widespread bipartisan public support. Special interest groups may oppose tax reform, for instance, although the simplification of the tax code and the elimination of tax expenditures that might make possible a simpler tax system with substantially lower marginal tax rates for all taxpayers. Other much-needed reforms impeded by special interest groups include entitlement spending, tort law, immigration policy, and student loans.

PROTECTING CAPITALISM FROM CRONYISM— BUSINESS'S SHARE OF THE JOB

There is an urgent need to combat crony capitalism, because if left unchecked it will continue to sap vitality out of the U.S. economy and undermine public support for the American model of capitalism. By all evidence, including public opinion polls and press accounts, many Americans believe that most or all of the business community is complicit in crony capitalism.[54] Crony capitalism has tarnished the reputation of business—deserved in some instances, but largely not. To change the terms of the debate on cronyism, the vast majority of business leaders who compete every day to provide jobs to their employees, investment opportunities to pension contributors and retirees, and high-value goods and services to all Americans and persons around the world, need to tell—and often to explain—the complex truth to their fellow citizens and their elected policymakers.

Moreover, business leaders need to practice the gospel of fair competition that they preach. As Alan Greenspan once said, we all want the fruits of vigorous competition among our suppliers and the providers of the goods and services we buy—we just don't want competition to apply to us. But if we all get the latter wish, there will be no competition, and our fate will be lower levels of innovation, productivity, and economic growth.

The first line of defense is awareness. That calls for making the case against cronyism so strongly that our society adopts an ingrained aversion to crony deals. Our elected policymakers should resist enacting additional deals and put a premium on efforts to reverse existing ones. And they should be rewarded by the voters for doing so. Conversely, business leaders should not seek crony deals.

Awareness includes making a distinction between what some economists call "pro-business" versus "pro-market" policies.[55] Supporting existing businesses through subsidies and preferential regulation to the detriment of new businesses and innovators distorts the market and does not contribute to long-term prosperity or economic growth. Truly "pro-market" policy is "pro-society" policy, which in the long term serves the interest of business and every other segment of our nation because it allows competition and markets to determine success or failure, and the ultimate allocation of resources.

So business must lead by example in rejecting crony capitalism. Business must also argue for reforms of Washington's ways to streamline policymaking, and reduce the influence of narrow interests. (We discuss those reforms in Chapter 5 of this book.) These steps are fundamental to building public confidence in capitalism from today's low ebb.

3

Focusing on Long-Term Value: Reversing Business Short-Termism

THE PRIMARY THREATS to sustaining capitalism are slow growth in productivity, income stagnation, and mounting public mistrust of leaders and institutions, both public and private. As we've seen, many forces contribute to these trends. But two related factors lie directly within the control of business leaders: the belief that businesses exist only to serve their owners, and business short-termism. These two phenomena are distinct, but clearly related.

The "shareholder-only model" is the relatively recent theory of business governance that businesses are responsible *only* to their owners and that business's sole purpose and responsibility is to maximize their owners' value.[56] These terms may sound like dry concepts out of a business textbook, but in fact they're critically important forces affecting how business decisions get made in the United States today.

One perspective is that the shareholder-primacy model is "arbitrarily and historically truncated along two axes: it is far too *narrow* and it is far too *shortsighted* . . . a responsible and prudent corporation of the twenty-first century must broaden its horizons beyond the economic interests of its shareholders to include the interests of the wider community that gave it birth and in which it would prosper."[57] Another perspective is that shareholder primacy implemented is a replay of the tragedy of the commons, depleting the resources that society needs to sustain itself.[58]

Business short-termism refers to the claim that owners (shareholders in the case of corporations), boards, and executives are too focused on short-term success and payoffs, at the expense of longer-term value and results. Business short-termism is causing real harm to capitalism's sustainability. In this chapter we'll catalogue some of those harms, describe the pressures driving corporate short-termism, and then propose solutions to turn the tide toward a more sustainable capitalism, including a return to a multi-stakeholder model of corporate governance. But first, let's briefly turn to a short history of how changes in our economy, corporations, and the larger society got us to where we find ourselves today.

A BRIEF HISTORY: CORPORATIONS IN THE U.S. ECONOMY SINCE WORLD WAR II

Changing beliefs: the shareholder–only model. In the decades following World War II, while their overseas competitors were busy rebuilding their war-ravaged economies, American businesses had the latitude of pursuing multiple goals, both social and economic.[59] Simultaneously scholars began advancing the idea that business's sole responsibility was to serve the corporation's shareholders and maximize profit. This "shareholder-only model" was in contrast to previous notions that business had broader responsibilities to the larger society. As early as 1962, economist Milton Friedman wrote, "there is but one and only one social responsibility of business—to use its resources and engage in activities designed to increase its profits so long as it stays within the rules of the game."[60]

Changing ownership. During this period the nature of corporate "owners"—the shareholders—was also changing, with large institutional shareholders like pension funds, insurance companies, and mutual funds becoming increasingly important. In the 1950s, large institutional shareholders held only 8 percent of U.S. corporations' stock. Today such shareholders own 67 percent of the outstanding stock of U.S. public corporations either directly or through outside asset managers, with the figure climbing to 70 percent for the 1,000 largest corporations.[61]

These large institutional shareholders share a number of characteristics. First, many, such as defined-benefit pension funds, tend to be long-term investors with long-time horizons due to the structure of their liabilities, which demand payments far into the future. Of course, many pension funds also pursue short-term gains or trading advantages, placing a portion of their resources with hedge funds and other money managers who trade with an eye for short-term profits. But at their core such institutions must pay attention to very long-term financial goals, as the lives of their beneficiaries extend decades.

Second, pension funds tend to be broadly diversified, either through their ownership of indexed funds or by directly indexing their holdings to certain benchmarks. In economic terms, these funds are so diversified that they do not stand to gain when one company outperforms another by shifting costs or profits in a zero-sum fashion: because their holdings are so diversified, they are likely to own shares of both. Rather, these large diversified shareholders tend to gain when companies expand productivity, thereby raising output, income, and cash flow in a positive-sum game.[62] So, too, do they gain when the economy is expanding and thereby creating the proverbial tide that lifts all boats.

Finally, some (though not all) large institutional shareholders, such as labor union pension funds or socially driven investors, are motivated to understand and influence decisions of companies they invest in—especially decisions with social or environmental impact. These can be both internal policies, such as hiring and diversity practices, and external ones, such as environmental or sourcing policies.

Changing public expectations. In recent decades, corporations have faced increasing public pressure to advance *social* goals beyond simply producing goods and services within the letter of the law and turning

SIDEBAR 3.1

Environmental, Social, and Governance (ESG) Considerations

Environmental, social, and governance (ESG) considerations frequently are taken as proxies for a company's attention to stakeholder interests. The two are not synonymous, but can overlap. Still, there is growing interest among U.S. institutional investors and asset managers in better understanding how to use ESG considerations in their investment decisions. The degree of adoption varies among investors who are incorporating ESG factors today. Most of these investors incorporate ESG considerations only in some asset classes or in some segmented or focused funds, not broadly across portfolios. *How* these investors adopt ESG varies too, as some use ESG as screening criteria (the way investors once screened "sin" stocks such as tobacco), while others apply ESG-based weightings as input decisions still largely based on financial performance, and still others have developed investment strategies targeting ESG trends.

Activists aside, corporate executives consistently say that questions about a company's social or environmental performance rarely come up in their conversations with large investors or analysts. Even many investors acknowledge that while the use of data on ESG factors has exploded—in 2014, Bloomberg reported a 76 percent year-over-year increase in customers using its ESG data—confidence in the data's relevance, accuracy, and usefulness continues to lag. Efforts to standardize environmental and social performance metrics remain embryonic. Initiatives to clarify ESG metrics and frameworks proliferate, adding to the confusion.

According to one estimate, since 1995 growth of assets under management guided by ESG considerations has outpaced the broader market for asset management in the United States. By 2012, ESG criteria were applied to $33 trillion (11.3 percent) of total assets under management in the United States. That was up 486 percent since 1995, versus the 386 percent growth of the total market for professionally managed funds during the same time period. In 2012, $1.54 trillion lay under the management of 200 institutional investors and asset managers that sponsored or co-sponsored shareholder resolutions addressing ESG issues.[63]

In a March 2015 study of institutional investors by Mercer and LGT Capital Partners, 75 percent of asset owners said they actively use ESG factors in investment decisions in alternative asset classes (such as private equity, real estate, and infrastructure—but not in their selection of hedge funds). Fifty-seven percent of them said they believed incorporating ESG factors has a positive impact on risk-adjusted returns. More than 50 percent of the institutional investors using ESG factors in investment considerations had adopted them just within the last three years. Respondents who do not use ESG criteria said that deficiencies in standardized ESG criteria and insufficient confidence in the relevance of ESG to investment decisions were the two chief barriers to adoption. Investors who use ESG criteria said greater clarity on techniques and strategies for incorporating ESG criteria would facilitate greater adoption across their portfolios. But they also said that there are too few asset managers they interview who incorporate ESG into their investment management processes.[64]

---

a profit at the end of the day. These higher public expectations cover a wide range of issues, including higher standards for corporate behavior and for product and service quality; increased attention to labor issues, including keeping more manufacturing jobs at home and not utilizing "sweatshops" overseas; greater concern for and protection of human rights and the environment; and greater attention to social goals, such as increasing diversity, investing in communities, or altering or eliminating products to reduce obesity. Labor groups, non-governmental organizations (NGOs), and consumer activists have carried out effective campaigns by bringing market and political pressure to bear on corporate targets in pursuit of such goals.

More than 70 percent of consumers and employees believe that companies can make decisions that both increase profits *and* improve economic and social conditions. They believe that CEOs and their companies could improve trust through greater engagement with constituencies, such as consumers, employees, and the public, and through more effective communication, and through demonstrations of integrity. And companies' performance in these areas can drive consumer behavior. Survey data indicate that a company's perceived effectiveness in these areas affects whether individuals say they will: buy a company's products or recommend them to others; pay a premium for products or services; choose to invest, speak, or write in support of a company's actions; and support or block its plans to locate in a community.[65]

Executives are feeling the heat, both to respond *and* to communicate what they are doing. Large, well-known companies including General Mills, McDonald's, Wal-Mart, The Gap, Apple, and Shell have phased out or altered their product ingredients, overhauled supplier strategies, altered investments, raised wages, and changed marketing or advertising practices. CEOs and the companies they lead are responding to rising stakeholder expectations, in part, because they believe that their customers (including those in their fastest-growing markets) and their employees care about how their companies conduct themselves. And companies want to "get the word out" about what they are doing. A majority of S&P 500 companies now report environmental and social performance metrics to investors and the larger public. Ten years ago, few did.[66]

The rise of "activist" investors and proxy advisory firms has helped drive this change. Some of these investors are focused primarily on increasing share value by slashing investments, cutting advertising, raising dividends, buying back stocks, or restructuring or selling off corporate units. But increasingly, some activist investors seek to advance environmental change, human rights, or other social goals by introducing shareholder resolutions to change company policies and strategies in these areas.

Of course, employees, labor unions, consumers, and advocates of social reform have sought to change the behavior of businesses and corporations throughout history—one need look no further than the period of labor unrest and "muckraking" at the end of the nineteenth and beginning of the twentieth centuries in the United States. Why does the ability of outside groups to exert pressure on corporations appear to have grown in recent years?

New communications technology is one key. Today companies exist in a world of 24-7 news cycles. Social media like Twitter and Facebook not only allow consumers and activists to disseminate their messages immediately and widely, but also to connect and build communities with likeminded individuals across broad geographies. Reputation has always been one of a company's most valuable assets. The difference today is that reputation can be severely damaged within hours or days by events that are difficult to predict. And the damage can spread seemingly instantaneously through communication channels that are so numerous they lie outside the control of any single organization or authority, whether that be a business or a government.

Low public trust in companies and business leaders, particularly in the wake of the financial crisis, helps to fuel the success of these campaigns. Each subsequent campaign or scandal that casts corporations or business leaders in a negative light breeds further public mistrust, which in turn makes it easier for future campaigns to succeed, in a downward cycle of growing public cynicism, stoked in part by those who benefit from it. Whereas many of the goals and outcomes of these campaigns have been positive, over time the cumulative diminishment of public trust in business and capitalism may threaten the system's overall viability.

Business Short-Termism

One negative result of "activist" owners and shareholders is short-termism: a focus on short-term results, often primarily or exclusively to benefit the shareholders. Top executives, members of corporate boards, and investors have grown alarmed that short-term pressures have crowded out longer-term planning and goals in corporations today. Sacrificing the long term to the short, they argue, can leave a legacy of suboptimal economic choices and lamentable underperformance. This temptation to profit in the short run—to eat the so-called seed corn now rather than save it to plant for the future—has been a constant challenge throughout human history. For example, a similar short-termism in the public sector has led elected officials to benefit at the ballot box over the short term through ongoing deficit-spending on entitlements and other federal programs while putting the nation's long-term fiscal health at risk.[67]

In the private sector, corporate leaders increasingly are concerned that short-term thinking is limiting the ability of companies to plan and invest in strategies that keep their businesses sustainable and vigorous. In 2013, 44 percent of top executives and corporate board members said their companies' planning horizons were less than three years, despite the fact that almost three-quarters believed that the horizon for planning strategy should extend beyond three years. An even larger 86 percent said they believed their companies' financial returns and innovation would improve if their strategies covered a longer time horizon.[68]

Costs of short-termism. Excessive focus on short-term benefits at the expense of long-term sustainability threatens capitalism both through reducing future growth in productivity and incomes, and through increased public cynicism.

- Quarterly earnings goals can create pressure to reduce short-term costs by laying off employees, reducing their training, or cutting other investment, especially in areas that do not show immediate returns, such as research and development (R&D). Corporate managers forgo otherwise profitable investments in order to "hit their numbers," thereby satisfying financial market expectations but giving up the opportunity to increase long-term company value.[69] Such actions affect employee attitudes, decision-making, motivation, and productivity. Ultimately the quality of goods or services the company produces may be affected. Reductions in R&D spending are particularly pernicious since this investment is most closely correlated with the overall economy's long-term productivity growth, one of the two ingredients of income growth over the long run.[70] In 2005, approximately 80 percent of chief financial officers said they would reduce discretionary spending on projects such as research and development to meet short-term earnings targets, and more than half said they would delay new projects even if it meant a sacrifice in value.[71]

- Comparing the investment behavior of privately held companies (which do not have to report quarterly earnings results) to that of publicly held companies (which do) lends support to the idea that pressure to meet quarterly earnings goals reduces investment. In one study, privately held companies invested nearly 10 percent of total assets per year, versus about 4 percent a year in comparable public companies. The study also found that private companies are more than three times as likely to invest in new opportunities compared to public companies.[72]

- Managing earnings in order to meet short-term goals misleads investors and misallocates capital. When the company exhausts the available short-term opportunities and the pipeline of future opportunities runs dry, a downward spiral can cause the company to be sold off.

- Excessively generous compensation of corporate managers, investment fund managers, and others for achieving financial targets that do not correspond to the creation of long-term economic value diverts business resources into the pockets of those individuals and away from activities and investments that do provide economic value and enhance the company's strength and viability.

- Excessive focus by professional money managers, such as those at mutual funds, on companies' short-term performance tends to lead to more active trading of the stocks in the fund. If the average mutual fund incurs an estimated 70–80 basis points of added costs from overactive trading, the resulting loss to investors would have amounted to about $60 billion to $70 billion in 2005 alone.[73]

- Another cost of short-termism may be the vibrancy of equity markets. When companies do not list on public exchanges, then their profit and value goes only to private owners and is not accessible to the general public to invest in. Since 1998, more than 300 companies have delisted from the NYSE and the number of companies listed on NASDAQ has dropped by about half. There are many reasons for the decline, but it's worth noting that during the last decade a number of companies, including Google and Facebook, have gone public with structures that allow executives and boards some defense against short-term pressures.[74]

Causes. If corporate short-termism carries such risk for the long-term interests of companies and the larger economy, how did it grow to be so pervasive? Research implicates a number of intertwined factors: incentive systems (both explicit and unstated), investor pressures, regulations, tax structures, financial metrics and accounting rules, trading technologies, and even business cultures and managerial mindsets.[75] Specifically:

- As noted above, the practice of providing quarterly earnings guidance leads financial actors, both inside and outside the corporation, to focus too heavily on reported earnings per share.

- Activist shareholders more frequently seek short-term interests than long-term ones. (Activists pressure for growth strategies only in one or two percent of instances, studies suggest.)[76] Between 2008 and 2015, activists led over 220 campaigns against U.S. companies to increase payouts to shareholders, most frequently through stock buybacks or cash returned to shareholders.[77] Such actions can drain the cash needed for long-term-value-increasing investment in physical capital and R&D, and harm the balance sheet and the long-term profitability of the firm.

- Many institutional investors, though their institutions nominally have a long-term investment focus, are in important ways short-term oriented. They measure the performance of their asset managers quarterly with short-term metrics and incentivize them to seek short-term performance. More broadly, their capital allocation and risk strategies may foster shorter-term investment behaviors within their organizations and in markets.[78]

- The structure of executive compensation can contribute to short-term outlooks by tying performance pay to the achievement of short-term financial targets.[79]

- Shortened tenures for CEOs naturally cause them to focus more on short-term results.[80] Some evidence indicates the incentive of CEOs to fund long-lived projects declines as they approach retirement or the end of a contract period.[81]

■ Changes in technology and regulation have reduced the cost of trading securities, thereby encouraging trading and changes in prices in response to each additional disclosure, each business development, and each burst of market activity. Many actors in the investment chain—asset managers, short-sellers, high-frequency traders, even some managers—opportunistically have sought to arbitrage market responsiveness without consideration for longer-term consequences.

The end result is the reality—or at the very least, a public perception—that some investors and executives are draining value from those companies in the short run, personally profiting from it, and then leaving the weakened companies—and the employees and communities that depend on them—behind to deal with the consequences.

Balancing the short and the long term. We do not advocate ignoring shareholders, or the need for short-term results, or the beneficial role that some activist investors play. Investors who are too entrenched can stifle productive change. One of the strengths of capitalism is that investment can move to its best and most effective uses in light of changes in technology, demand, and the effectiveness of an enterprise's management. Investors can withdraw their capital from companies that are not managing for the future effectively. The challenge, of course, is for investors to be able to discern when a company's poor financial performance in the present presages deeper future problems versus when that poor performance is simply a temporary blip or the result of management appropriately incurring costs in the present to enhance the company's future performance and sustainability.

It is challenging to strike the right balance between the short and the long term, especially given that directors and managers typically must make decisions under high levels of uncertainty arising from sources both external and internal to the company. Uncertainty about the future of government fiscal, monetary, and regulatory policies is one source of uncertainty. Changes in markets, technology, and other economic events present another set of challenges. The flexibility of directors and managers to make quick decisions in response to such changes and manage the associated risks is a strength of the U.S. economy that should not be underrated or lightly discarded.

What are corporate leaders to do in light of the grave harms of corporate short-termism, the set of pressures driving companies in this direction, and the admitted difficulty of striking the right balance between long- and short-term goals? Although we recognize the challenge of the situation, there are steps that corporate leaders—both members of corporate boards and executives—can take to move their companies toward greater focus on long-term sustainability, thereby benefiting not only their companies, but also the sustainability of capitalism as a whole.

SOLUTIONS: LONG-TERM VALUE CREATION THROUGH THE MULTI-STAKEHOLDER MODEL

First, it should be recognized that corporate leaders do not have complete control over whether their companies will focus primarily on long- or short-term goals. Corporations operate in free markets to obtain the capital investment they need to do business. If investors systematically prefer companies that pursue short-term goals—such as maximizing quarterly earnings—then companies that try to do otherwise may lose capital relative to those that do. Investors—or an activist subset of investors—who are looking for quick profits may even replace managers who focus on a longer time horizon. Just as voters decide whether our elected leaders take a long- or short-term view, so too do investors ultimately determine whether corporations are managed for short-term gains or longer-term sustainability. Democracies get the leaders they deserve. In free markets, corporations pursue the strategies that investors will support.

However, having acknowledged that ultimately investors are paramount, the reality remains that corporate leadership—both executives and boards of directors—must work with investors to counter corporate short-termism given their direct knowledge and control of companies in the present. True leaders will take these steps to ensure the long-term viability of their firms, even if it puts them at risk from those who seek short-term gain at the expense of long-term sustainability.

To counter corporate short-termism, business leaders should convincingly communicate the firm's objectives and time horizons, tie performance metrics for the firm and for executive compensation to them, and communicate the company's goals and performance clearly to all concerned, including the general public.

State the firm's objectives and time horizon. Each firm should affirmatively decide the time horizon over which it seeks to maximize and maintain value and articulate the right balance among its various stakeholders including customers, employees, the community, the environment, and other relevant entities.[82]

We strongly believe that firms should choose a multi-stakeholder approach to value creation and aim for maintenance of value over the long term. Adopting a long-term perspective leads naturally to a multi-stakeholder approach since companies *cannot* prosper over the longer term without taking appropriate care of their customers, employees, suppliers, the environment, and the communities in which they do business.

We recognize that a challenge of the multi-stakeholder approach is that it involves setting priorities and executing tradeoffs. The board and the CEO must find ways to express which stakeholders stand at what place in the line of priorities, and over what time horizons. And those priorities must be more than mere statements of good intentions. The actions undertaken must go beyond defensive moves aimed merely at minimizing risks to the stakeholder or improving the firm's reputation. Authentic approaches to incorporating stakeholders into value creation tend to be proactive, rooted in core culture and strategy, transparent, and oriented toward increasing stakeholder value along with long-term business value. GE's Ecomagination initiative, Unilever's sustainable growth strategy, and IBM's Smarter Planet platform are examples of creative efforts in this regard. A straightforward short-term approach that only recognizes shareholder value is

On Corporate Boards: Every Other One a Woman

As corporate boards oversee their organization's shift toward more sustainable business strategies, they also need to confront another critical piece of this change agenda: the composition of the board itself. Specifically, U.S. corporate boards must step up efforts to integrate women leaders into boardrooms.

Women comprise more than one-half the population in the United States, more than one-half the work force, and earn more than one-third of MBA degrees conferred by the nation's business schools. Nielsen says that women account for the greater share of spending today in nearly every retail-shopping category, and the Boston Consulting Group has estimated that increased spending controlled by or influenced by women, globally, will grow bigger and faster than spending by China's and India's combined rising middle class.

In other words, whereas women represent a significant portion of stakeholders—customers, employees, owners, suppliers, and communities—women occupy less than 19 percent of Fortune 500 board seats today, according to a study by Catalyst. That percentage has grown less than six percentage points (from 13.6 percent to 19 percent) in the last decade. At this rate it will take many decades for board membership to reflect gender parity with the economy at large. This disparity is inconsistent with a board's desire to utilize all sources of expertise and insight for its deliberations, as one means for a company to compete effectively in the global marketplace. The scarcity of women leaders on boards also raises questions about how well corporations utilize their human capital, about the business consequences of potentially alienating female constituents, and the insensitivity this seems to suggest to stakeholders about the company's ability to follow impor-tant social trends on gender issues.

The impediment to progress is a "chicken and egg" problem. Board nominating committees, their consultants, search firms, and corporate executives tend to prefer to consider new director candidates who are either sitting or retired CEOs, or current directors of other companies. Women are a small minority of these groups today, and hence the pool is unnecessarily limited. The criteria for potential director candidates should be broader—other female C-suite executives (not just CEOs), financial service executives, entrepreneurs, accounting firm partners, or foundation heads. In annual proxy statements, nominating committees profess a desire for board diversity, but tend to repeat customary behaviors, which ipso facto discourage diversity, in a self-perpetuating cycle.

Boards should set publicly disclosed goals for increasing board diversity. To achieve these targets, boards should re-think the criteria for directors and consider a broader range of women leaders as potential candidates. Corporate directors and business leaders should also step up efforts to encourage their peers to demand real progress in board diversity. If boards replaced every other retiring director with a woman, they could close the gap by 10 percentage points in just a few years. So, why not adopt a new practice: make every other new board member a woman. Every other one.

---

simpler, of course. But it is inferior because it risks the firm's very survival over the long run.

Align performance metrics and incentives to the firm's goals. Boards should tie a portion of compensation, for the CEO and other senior managers, to their performance against metrics operationally tied to the corporation's governing objectives. This will incentivize top management to pay attention to multi-constituent relations, reputation, and long-term value creation. It also would require the corporation to disclose the link between performance pay and the chosen benchmarks.[83]

The board would have to choose and track the types of information it would need to evaluate the CEO's performance.[84] For example, if a company's strategic plan emphasizes research and development as a contributor to long-term value, its compensation plan ought to link rewards to success in R&D. Other examples of criteria might be employee retention, customer satisfaction, or adaptability to changes in public policies. There surely are many more.[85]

Compensation should also be tied to whatever time frame the firm chooses. For example, if a firm chooses a five-year time horizon then some of an executive's compensation should be based on the firm's performance five years hence.

Communicate, communicate, communicate. In today's world of open communications, where a plethora of information (including the inaccurate) about corporations is available to anyone, corporations that wish to survive must pursue transparency, by making accurate, honest, and insightful public disclosures of their activities and motivations.

In the context of our broader recommendations for a long-term multi-constituency approach, a firm's objectives and principles must be communicated clearly. The firm's priorities will have no impact on its behavior and on the reactions of its stakeholders if they are secret or misunderstood. As is commonly noted, communication is a two-way street: companies need to seek and truly listen to the input of their stakeholders.

Too few companies have developed a set of metrics that investors can use to understand and monitor long-term value creation at that particular firm. Examples might include long-term economic value added, R&D efficiency, patent pipelines, multi-year return on capital investments, and energy intensity of production.[86] Companies also could communicate their long-term visions for the business and components of their long-term strategic plan. In a 2014 survey of 772 corporate directors, conducted by McKinsey & Company, half of the directors said that "regularly communicating the company's long-term strategy and performance to key long-term shareholders would be one of the most effective ways to alleviate the pressure to maximize short-term returns and stock prices."[87] Business leaders and boards of directors need to lead the changes that will create value for a wider set of stakeholders, and to re-balance short-term performance relative to long-term value creation.

In recent years a number of companies have developed more systematic processes for identifying critical stakeholders and for building two-way communication with them. At Alcoa, for instance, national or even local business units incorporate a "public strategy" in their business plans. Following defined company-wide standards and tools for interacting with stakeholders, business unit leaders identify key local stakeholder groups, learn to understand the issues that are important to them, anticipate potential friction points, and establish standardized Alcoa mechanisms (such as town hall meetings, plant walk-throughs, or newsletters) for ongoing, fact-based communications with multiple constituencies. Many of Alcoa's local units have established community advisory panels that also host public forums to obtain stakeholder input. Alcoa has found that it can resolve most stakeholder issues at the local level. Alcoa and other companies also partner with NGOs, in some instances, to ensure that the needs of the groups represented by the NGOs are being addressed.

Maintaining a focus on long-term sustainability will need to be a conscious decision reached by executives, boards, investors, and all stakeholders. It is easy to pursue short-term gain at the expense of long-term sustainability. That is why true business leaders must speak out on the importance of building and maintaining enduring value—for their institutions, and for the people and communities that depend on them. And that true leadership—over time—will help restore the American public's frayed trust in those institutions and in capitalism itself.

4

Reform Education

ENHANCING OUR EDUCATIONAL SYSTEM lies at the heart of making capitalism sustainable, because education provides tools for boosting individual productivity and social mobility. From a national perspective, increasing American workers' productivity would help to accelerate the recent stagnant growth in our national income, thereby expanding the size of the collective economic "pie" and making the other challenges facing capitalism easier to solve. From an individual perspective, education remains the best path up the income ladder. The key to upward mobility in today's (and tomorrow's) knowledge-based economy is and will increasingly be the ability to do a job or provide value that can't be done by a machine, robot, or computer.

Business leaders have been calling for reform of our public education system for decades, concerned by the steadily widening gap between what students learn (or not) in schools and the skills that employers of all kinds need in today's work environments. They haven't been the only ones raising alarms. Surveys have shown mounting concern among college and university faculty. Over the years, fewer and fewer university professors have believed America's K12 education system is adequately preparing students to succeed in post-secondary classrooms. Leaders of two- and four-year colleges decry the increasing amounts their institutions spend on remedial teaching for unprepared students. [88]

Executives understand the importance of education. They see it in their hiring metrics (jobs unfilled because they can't find the right employees, or filled outside the United States) and, for many of them, rising remedial employee-training costs. Businesses are the primary "consumer" of the output of our education system. Leaders of global businesses anecdotally see it in the higher quality of new graduates in other nations in which they operate—mirrored by findings of multi-nation tests of student skills. Executives understand the importance of education to society, specifically the link between education and upward mobility, and its importance to our civic health. Many companies support education projects through foundations or corporate social responsibility initiatives. Many executives personally involve themselves in educational institutions, or fund social sector organizations that experiment with new educational approaches.

There is a clear nexus between the quality of a country's education system and a variety of social and economic indicators. As discussed in Chapter 1, higher levels of educational attainment correlate with improved social outcomes and higher productivity. Education is also the *sine qua non* of equal opportunity—it's what makes it possible for people from all backgrounds to compete equally. But with so many shortcomings in the education system, identifying reforms that will improve educational outcomes and equalize opportunity can pose a challenge for business and policy leaders.

The solution to this challenge lies in three areas: (1) additional investment and attention to early care and education of children ages 0–5; (2) significant reform to the U.S. K12 public education system, which forms the core platform for building skills; and (3) a re-thinking of national goals for post-secondary education and workforce development.

Education is an important public good that warrants a government role and both public and private funding, especially for the most disadvantaged members of our society. Public financing of education for all children, from kindergarten through high school at a minimum, is a foundational investment society must make in itself. But how education is *paid for* and how it is *delivered* can be separated, and in some instances should be, to foster more competition and improve outcomes.

In our view, expanding access to higher quality education at the lowest cost at all levels requires competition and market mechanisms in the delivery of education. Reform must focus on *outcomes* (e.g., what students know and can do) rather than *inputs* (e.g., number of teachers or schools or courses taught) or even *outputs* (e.g., the number of degrees conferred)—because ultimately only outcomes really matter to individuals and families, businesses, and the economy. To succeed, reform also must make the U.S. educational system more transparent at every level, with easily accessible information and metrics that matter. The remainder of this chapter advocates specific solutions at each level of education: early childhood, K12, and post-secondary education. Each level forms an important part of a comprehensive whole.

INVEST IN EARLY CHILDHOOD EDUCATION

Early learning sets the foundation for developing our nation's human capital. Research findings consistently have shown a high return on investment (ROI) for high-quality programs serving disadvantaged children.[89] Research also shows that high-quality early childhood care and education strengthen families, communities, and economic development.[90] Advocates for early education programs (including the CED) have pushed for increased funding for early education; access to high-quality early childhood education for all children, ages 0–5, particularly those in greatest need; high standards for early childhood programs and teachers; family engagement in education and development; full-day kindergarten programs; and improving the quality of education in grades 1–3 to sustain children's gains from early education.[91]

Public and private investment in early education has followed the research findings and advocacy. The good news is that over the last 15 years, the number of state-funded preschool "slots"—that is, openings or available spots for individual children—has increased steadily, nearly

FIGURE 4.1   Preschool Participation of Four-Year-Olds by Socioeconomic Status (SES) Quintile

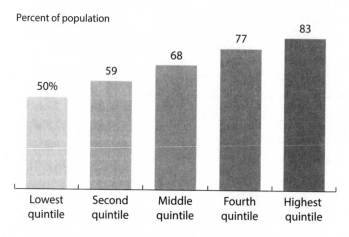

Percent of population

Source: Grover J. (Russ) Whitehurst and Ellie Klein, "Do we already have universal preschool?" Evidence Speaks Reports, Vol 1, #1, Economic Studies at Brookings, September 17, 2015 (https://www.brookings.edu/wp-content/uploads/2016/06/Evidence-Speaks-Report-vol1.pdf).

doubling the percentage of four-year-olds enrolled in pre-kindergarten programs. Today, with 29 percent of four-year-olds enrolled in state-funded programs, another 10 percent of four-year-olds served by Head Start, and 3 percent in special education programs, about 42 percent of the nation's four-year-olds attend publicly funded preschools.[92] Overall, a recent analysis found that 69 percent of children entering kindergarten in 2010–2011 had attended a preschool program, either public or private, the previous year.[93] But the chances a four-year-old attends preschool is closely related to his or her family income. Over three-quarters of four-year-olds from the most well-to-do families attend preschool, compared to only half of four-year-olds from families in the lowest socioeconomic quintile (see Figure 4.1).

Additional publicly funded slots for low-income families can help close the gap. Today, the number of families desiring state-funded pre-kindergarten slots exceeds those available in most U.S. communities, but funding for these programs generally has plateaued since 2010. Moreover, funding for educational opportunities for children younger than four years old has been, and remains, inadequate. Although many governors, both Republican and Democratic, voice interest in expanding state funding for early childhood education, ongoing state and federal budget pressures make the outlook for significant further growth in public early childhood expenditures challenging.[94] Because education is primarily a state and local government responsibility, almost by definition the parts of the country that need early education opportunities the most can afford them the least.

It's essential to increase the availability of high-quality early care and education. For example, state governments should consider providing direct support of early education to families via vouchers, allowing parents to choose a provider of early childhood education. The federal government, state governments, foundations, and other private organizations also should support ongoing experimentation and research into how to maximize the effectiveness of investments in early education, seeking to better understand which early education programs or practices work best, why, and how to scale them. Findings on effective practices should be disseminated widely in user-friendly formats to providers, families, and the public at large. All studies and evaluations of early learning programs also should collect data on the costs involved in providing programs and services, to improve understanding of the ROI of scaled-up programs as they operate under real-world conditions.

K12 EDUCATION: FOCUS ON THE LEARNING TRIAD

U.S. elementary and secondary schools—or "K12" for short—lie at the center of our educational system. Universal education through high school was a twentieth-century American innovation that contributed enormously to the "American century."[95] The United States offers a free education from kindergarten through 12th grade at public expense for every child. Approximately 87 percent of K12 students were enrolled in public schools in 2013–2014, and private schools served 9 percent.[96] By a wide consensus Americans believe that everyone ideally *should* complete at least a high school education, even if some do not go on to post-secondary education. By the 2011–2012 school year, 81 percent of students who entered high school as freshmen four years earlier had graduated, up from 71 percent in 1995–1996.[97]

As many business and policy leaders and educators have long argued, graduation rates alone are not an adequate measure of learning. For instance, the reading and math skills possessed by a *majority* of the nation's students graduating from a public high school fall short of what they need to succeed in a college classroom or in many workplaces today, according to the 2015 findings of the National Assessment of Educational Progress—an assessment shared by many employers.[98] Both the private and the public sectors, including workplaces, community and four-year colleges, and universities, bear the cost of remediating these skill deficiencies. In the worst case—when the deficiency isn't remediated—the cost is shared by the individual, who experiences a lifetime of reduced earnings and opportunities, and by society, in the form of increased spending on the social safety net.

The United States *must* do better. Improved outcomes in K12 schools will require concerted and systematic improvement in three intersecting areas: boosting student readiness, driving improved teacher quality, and raising the bar on the quality of *what* is taught.[99] All three elements are important. And all three elements can and should be targets of policy and reform to achieve our ultimate goal of improved student outcomes. Unfortunately the nation's current fights over testing have distracted us from what needs to be done.

Avoiding the red herring of testing disputes. Tests are overemphasized by both advocates and critics of today's educational system. They are simply tools—in part to measure the extent to which the country, states, school districts, and schools are achieving the ultimate goal of student learning. However, tests are important. In the short term, classroom tests give teachers and students immediate feedback and allow them to "correct course" if the student is not mastering the material. Over the longer term, summative tests covering a larger scope of material allow for *management* at the school and system level and *accountability* at the school, system, and higher levels. All of these functions—feedback, management, and accountability—contribute to student learning, so it is difficult to imagine an effective education system without testing. But if we really want to improve learning and student outcomes, we need to focus on the three elements of the learning triad: students, teachers, and what is taught.

Helping students to be ready to learn. Health, motivation, ability to focus, and aptitude all affect how much students *can* learn once they arrive in the classroom. Many factors affect a child or young person's ability to learn, including the level of support for learning in the child's home, peer pressure, and the positive or negative influence of the neighborhood in which a student lives. Although there are myriad opinions on what enhances a child's readiness to learn, business and policy leaders should focus investments and policies on approaches that hard evidence suggests are effective. For instance, high-quality, early-childhood programs, as discussed above, enhance the ability of students to benefit from their classroom experiences in subsequent years. Much has been learned about the components of model programs that have real impact on children and families' lives. Businesses, nonprofits, and religious organizations can and should step up to replicate these models.[100]

Teacher quality. Efforts to raise the quality of K12 teachers should focus on improving the way school systems select faculty, evaluate their performance, provide for their professional development, and design their compensation and benefits plans. Teachers should be treated as the professionals they are. That means giving them greater decision-making authority, and in turn holding them accountable to high performance standards. Compensation plans and pension systems for teachers, along with career paths, should be designed to attract and retain the most highly qualified teachers while also ensuring their accountability to the public.

To that end, teachers' compensation should be based in part on evaluations of their on-the-job performance, as measured both quantitatively and qualitatively by student learning. Compensation also should reflect that recruiting and retaining qualified teachers varies by field, since some fields (e.g., math and science) provide competitive opportunities for teachers outside the classroom. Similarly, teacher compensation should include incentives for effective teachers to take and remain in positions at hard-to-staff schools.[101]

School districts also should design career paths so that good teachers don't have to leave the classroom for administrative positions to boost their salaries. Finally, policymakers must lead the charge to improve teacher evaluation and compensation systems, strengthen data systems, expand incentives for districts to experiment with new forms of teacher compensation, provide sustainable school funding, and engage wide stakeholder involvement.

Standards, standards, standards. No matter how ready and able students are to learn, and teachers to teach, the content of what is taught must be relevant to what the student needs to succeed after graduation. States should adopt college- and career-ready standards that allow their students to compete at the highest level in the global economy and align high-quality curricula, materials, and yes, tests, to those standards.

Much mischief has been made in political and policy debates by those who intentionally or unintentionally confuse educational standards, curriculum, and the testing associated with them. Standards are written frameworks that describe in a fairly detailed way the minimum level of knowledge and skills students at different grade levels should master.[102] Curriculum refers to *what* is taught—specific topics—and *how*, for instance via written text, activities, online or material. Standards describe the desired goal. Curricula are the ways of reaching that goal. Appropriately designed tests help us know whether we got there.

In the United States, the responsibility for developing education standards falls to the states, although local districts often supplement and expand upon the state standards. Through the early 2000s, states developed their own standards for K12 education. Starting with the passage of the federal No Child Left Behind law in 2001, states were required to test students annually in English language arts and math in grades 3–8 using tests aligned to the state standards.[103] Schools that failed to make "adequate yearly progress" toward the goal of having 100 percent of students proficient on the tests by 2014 faced sanctions. Given this set of incentives, many states chose non-rigorous standards, non-rigorous state tests, or both.[104]

Many leaders in state government, education, and business recognized these deficiencies. In 2009, a coalition of groups led by the National Governors Association and the Council of Chief State School Officers launched an effort to develop a set of rigorous standards for K12 mathematics and English language arts that states could voluntarily adopt and that would be aligned with the knowledge and skills needed for college and work. These standards became known as the Common Core State Standards. Ultimately, 45 states and the District of Columbia adopted the Common Core (although three states subsequently rescinded their adoption).[105]

The importance of *shared* standards is often neglected. The United States represents a single, integrated national economy. Yet if a high school diploma requires varying levels of skills across different states, it makes the credential less meaningful for employers and makes it more difficult for graduates of "low-rigor" states to compete for jobs in states with higher standards. In our highly mobile society, it helps if the same content is being taught at the same grade level in most states. Otherwise a child moving between states risks repeating the same material twice, or, worse, missing some topics entirely, just because one state teaches that material in 4th grade while another teaches it in the 5th grade.

CED firmly supports the Common Core State Standards, but if states find that they cannot adopt the Common Core for whatever reason, they should adopt globally competitive college- and career-ready standards, whatever name they give them. Then, equally importantly, they should align high-quality curricula, materials, and tests to those standards at the school, school district, or state level. The development of a wide variety of curricula and materials should be encouraged, as long as they are aligned with a shared set of rigorous standards.

POST–SECONDARY EDUCATION AND WORKFORCE DEVELOPMENT

Reforms of post-secondary education and worker training should focus on remediating the high cost of higher education, the misalignment between the skills acquired to earn a degree and those needed to succeed in the job market, and the shortage of resources needed to re-skill workers for new jobs in a dynamic economy. Real reform should be based on the principle that workers at every level will need lifelong learning, and that this can occur within a wide variety of venues and formats.

Although there are many goals for post-secondary education—such as exposure to the liberal arts and preparing students to be better citizens—business leaders are best positioned to focus primarily on education's role in preparing students for employment. Having a highly skilled workforce is a public good because the U.S. economy as a whole benefits when skills improve. By focusing on *workforce development* in its broadest sense, reform efforts can be directed at improving needed skills rather than simply the number of post-secondary degrees awarded. A focus on workforce development rather than college degrees also emphasizes the lifetime nature of adult learning. Many young men and women in the workforce today will change jobs and even careers multiple times during their working lives and will need continuous re-skilling. A "one-and-done" mindset with regard to earning a post-secondary degree is already outdated.

Traditional structures and boundaries of learning must be flexible. Education for adult, "non-traditional" students—many of whom have families and may have worked for many years—must be structured differently from traditional two- and four-year courses of study. Similarly, preparing young people for well-paying, satisfying jobs ideally should begin well before high school ends. High school and even middle school is not too early to help students explore meaningful career choices. Career academies, for instance, which link apprenticeships with education in the related academic skills, provide a path to employment and also help students understand the relevance of what they are learning in the classroom. Solid grounding in fundamental skills should begin at even younger ages. The math skills necessary for lucrative and much-in-demand STEM (science, technology, engineering, and math) jobs must begin in elementary school, or even earlier.

Chief among reforms needed to achieve workforce development is greater transparency, particularly of costs and outcomes in the market for post-secondary education. Efforts to improve transparency also should aim to give consumers and others greater clarity regarding the *competencies* students achieve. Delivery of post-secondary education, unlike K12, is with some exceptions a free market in the United States. Students and families typically pay for their own post-secondary education, although significant government subsidies and some private scholarships exist. Many universities receive significant public subsidies. Generally, this has created a "marketplace" for obtaining post-secondary education and training, with a variety of providers and models. But the market is fraught with distortions, including serious information gaps. Students and families can obtain some information about the true price families can expect to pay at particular colleges after financial aid,[106] about the labor market value of particular majors,[107] and about the relative value-added of particular colleges.[108] In the near future, the development of more comprehensive information in colleges and universities may enable us to predict the likelihood that a student with a particular set of academic and personal characteristics will complete various courses of study. Similarly, increasingly sophisticated statewide longitudinal data systems that can track individuals' education and workforce outcomes up through their 20s, will make it possible in some states to predict the likely earnings of someone graduating from a particular public college or university with a particular degree.

What's crucially absent is information about *outcomes*: what skills, knowledge, and competencies do students acquire by the end of their program? What did the college (or course) contribute to this learning? That is, what is the institution's value-add (as opposed to things the student would have learned regardless of attending the institution)? In short, what do students *learn* in their various post-secondary activities?

Colleges and students make claims about what students have learned in college, but employers' ratings of those skills are different. For example, 62 percent of recent college graduates feel they are well prepared in oral communication skills, but only 28 percent of employers agree. This pattern is consistent across a broad range of workforce-relevant skills.[109] One relatively recent study administered a particular test—the Collegiate Learning Assessment—to a large sample of students at the beginning and end of their college careers, and made waves when it found that most students achieved only minor improvements in critical thinking and written communication during their time in college.[110]

If students and their families had better information about what they were buying in the "marketplace" for post-secondary education, there would be more competition among institutions of higher learning, more innovation, reductions in cost, and higher-quality outcomes. Students also need information on the knowledge and competencies employers need and demand. Existing tools for this, such as the Occupational Information Network (O*NET), funded by the U.S. Department of Labor (which provides highly detailed information on the "skills, abilities, knowledge, tasks, work activities, work context, experience levels required, job interests, work values/needs, and work styles" for over 900 occupations), do not reach the level of a fully functioning market.

In many ways employers are primary drivers of our post-secondary education system through the characteristics for which they choose to hire. Although students and their families are the primary consumers of post-secondary education, employers are also important because they hire the "output" of the system (graduates) as their workers. Many employers hire on the basis of the educational degree obtained or the school attended—using these as a proxy for an applicant's competencies. Although these characteristics provide some signal of what an individual knows and is able to do on the job, they're not exactly the same. Many individuals may have developed the same skills through other avenues, such as military service or running their own business. And there are valid and reliable assessments of many of these skills. To the extent that employers engage in greater competency-based hiring, it will help drive post-secondary institutions of all types, including some that do not even exist today, to do a better job of teaching students the skills and knowledge they need to obtain good jobs. Greater use of such assessments will give students a clear understanding of what's needed to obtain and advance in particular jobs. These assessment also will aid employers in communicating job requirements clearly to job applicants. Applied to existing staff, reliable competency assessments could help employers to identify competency gaps and areas in need of focused training. Over the longer term, this would improve the efficiency of the market for post-secondary education.

Consider that data and predictive analytics could be used to advise incoming "students" (and other consumers of workforce development programs) of the probability that someone with their characteristics will complete the degree program they are considering, and the likelihood of their finding employment (and expected earnings) following completion of the program or degree. This, combined with information about the cost of the program, would allow students to make more informed decisions about the value of pursuing a particular course of study. More sophisticated versions of such analytics could suggest alternative courses of study to individual students that could lead to improved outcomes for the student in question. This kind of personalized advising is clearly feasible for most post-secondary institutions, especially to the extent that they can link to data on their former students' employment outcomes.

■ ■ ■

Education is central to ensuring both our nation's overall prosperity, and the upward social mobility that is a hallmark of capitalism and contributes to its social acceptance. Ensuring that the U.S.'s educational system helps to level the playing field and is tailored to the rising demands of the twenty-first century global economy is critical to capitalism's sustainability. Enacting the recommendation contained in this chapter will help to meet those goals.

Business leaders must begin to communicate the urgency of reform in early childhood education, K12 public education, and workforce development. They can articulate and champion education reform at every level. But their most immediate and direct impact should be on improving workforce development. Businesses will have an evolving role to play in supporting workers' access to, and pursuit of, post-secondary education and skills development. Employers can form alliances with organizations that educate and train the future workforce in their communities. They can also play an active role in advocating policies and pathways to more affordable, market-aligned skills attainment for workers of all ages. They can provide flexible scheduling that allows adult learners to balance work and education. And they can implement on-the-job mentorships and training that accelerate skill development.

Business leaders should urge policymakers to ensure that government continues its important role in subsidizing post-secondary education, training, and retraining for America's most disadvantaged individuals— and for those who have lost their jobs due to global competition. Policymakers should also dismantle regulatory barriers and disincentives to innovative approaches to workplace development—for instance, rules that make it difficult for students to obtain federal loan aid for programs that are not based on credit hours.

Implementing these reforms to all three levels of education will require concerted public and private leadership over the long term. Reform is needed critically. Business leaders have been at the forefront of education reform for many years, but now is the time for them to double-down on their efforts. Education is foundational to equality of opportunity, and absent significant reform of how and what students and workers in this nation learn, the American dream of upward mobility, national competitiveness, and the sustainability of capitalism all are at risk.

5

Making Washington Work

MAKING CAPITALISM SUSTAINABLE requires a well-functioning government, unencumbered by the taint of partisanship and the influence of money. Washington is far from that state today. The undue influence that money and lobbying—the tools of crony capitalism—can wield in Washington is harmful to the economy and to public trust. But those tools also can undermine the integrity and effectiveness of the policymaking process itself. Those forces have collapsed what we call *The Vital Center*—the core of our elected leadership who are willing to put partisanship aside to seek the common good. The outcome is a process that arrives at what often appear to be—and likely are—unfair and ill-considered outcomes.

Our nation's broad agreement on the need to work toward consensus on public issues has been a fundamental contributor to America's long-term prosperity. But today, the political class in Washington has degenerated to the point where civic debate has become uncivil invective; analysis has been displaced by ideology; and problems are not solved, but rather stored for future partisan use. The breakdown of the political process in Washington poses a real threat to the consensual foundation of our nation's prosperity. America's elected leaders as well as the country's major political institutions have lost the public trust, and thus the ability to govern. This inability to govern means business—and workers and our entire economy—will suffer.

A number of crucial issues are already going unaddressed: the rising accumulation of public debt; still-growing and potentially crippling health care costs; a looming Social Security shortfall; an education system that leaves too many of our children behind world standards; and the impact of globalization, technology, and stagnating wages on a substantial number of U.S. workers. This inaction in the face of crisis is a disgrace of monumental proportions. A government that cannot confront these visible challenges will surely lack the reserves of comity and trust to face any unknown and sudden—perhaps even more dangerous—crises.

Many well-intentioned members of Congress talk publicly about the breakdown of the political process, and many promise reform. However, partisan debate has become so rancorous that it is a threat to the country's firms, customers, employees, owners, voters, and ultimately to our very democracy. Without significant reform of the legislative process itself (coupled with reforms to campaign funding and lobbying) it is hard to see how the country's institutions can deal with this crisis.

In short, if the country's democracy cannot make itself sustainable, then the country's capitalist system cannot be sustainable. Similarly, the American ideal and American prosperity both will die. We hold our future in our own hands.

In the past, business leaders have spoken out honestly and openly about addressing public issues. Today, the erosion of public trust in virtually all institutions—including but not limited to business—has cowed many business leaders into silence. The result is a state of suspended trust, and silent business leaders cannot regain the public trust. The American people know sincerity and concern for the public interest when they see it. We urge our fellow business men and women to climb out of the foxhole and step into the public square to advocate reasoned solutions in the nation's interest, rather than either partisan politics or self-interest. This entails risk, and rebuilding the public trust will not be quick or easy. But without such risk, everything that is exceptional about the United States is at even greater risk. The workings of Washington are central to our success as a nation in every area of public policy. This may be one of the best starting points for business leaders to take action to make capitalism sustainable.

Flawed Processes and Broken Procedures

The enormous sums of money injected into the political process by various interest groups—along with the seemingly increased influence some interests have had on outcomes—have weakened both the motivation for, and the practice of, consensus-seeking in the legislative process. Additionally, many politicians abuse redistricting to protect incumbents and radically reduce the number of competitive seats—by both political parties—which is choking the political process in Washington. There are numerous flaws in the way business is transacted in Washington in the legislative process itself, generating unfortunate outcomes.

Business leaders must use their public platforms to advocate needed fixes in the public sector. This is not exerting "undue influence." As outlined throughout this book, the efficiency of free markets is diminished when government's role in the economy is unnecessarily interventionist. Reform to make the U.S. economy more productive should focus on two primary areas: the burden of the national debt should be reduced by bringing federal spending and revenue into line; and an outdated, creaky regulatory system must be streamlined. Reforms in these areas will bring greater dynamism to the U.S. economy and help ensure the sustainability of capitalism.

Solutions for reforming these two substantive areas of policy follow. However, the solutions begin with the very workings of Washington itself. The policymaking process has all but stopped working, stalled in partisanship and rancor, and corrupted by the influence of expensive and unending re-election campaigns. The roots of Washington's dysfunction lie in crony capitalism and the disappearance of a vital center from the legislative process.

Washington must be made to work again. Limiting the size of government and its role in the economy in the right way will reduce the stakes—and the opportunities—for special interests to spend money to influence policy, without penalizing the American people. Curtailing government intervention is a theme throughout this book, and it will be facilitated by reducing public spending and the deficit, reforming the tax system, and streamlining regulatory policies. Before this can happen, elected leaders from both parties must once again work toward a consensus about the legislative process itself. The objectives and nonpartisan steps in the following section can markedly improve our nation's governance, and its public-policy outcomes.

Reform Campaign Finance

The 2016 presidential campaign provided a couple of new twists to old campaign financing truisms. One political party's candidate cleverly used the television news cycle and social media to get free—and greater—exposure than his competitors, thereby dramatically lowering his overall campaign expenses. A candidate running in the other party used the Internet to raise small donations from millions of contributors, amassing enormous funds to fuel traditional campaign expenditures, such as television advertising. It is too early to tell whether either of these tactics proves to be a harbinger of new trends in political campaigning, or merely an anomaly. Regardless, they are reminders that money, and lots of it, fuels political campaigns, particularly in federal elections. The aim of reform should be to free elected officials from their dependence on the continuous cycle of private campaign funding.

The playing field between small and large campaign contributions should be leveled by implementing a system of matching funds. For instance, public financing might match the first $250 of every campaign donation, perhaps by a multiple of as much as four to one. This would make small donations more valuable to a campaign, which might induce candidates to put more effort into pursuing small donations, and connecting with a greater number of voters. It might also allow candidates to achieve a competitive level of finance solely through benign small contributions, the sheer numbers of which would make exploiting them to influence candidates for personal gain either highly unlikely or impossible.

CED supports the matching-fund option to increase the opportunities to publicly fund campaigns. Other authorities have offered different ideas.[111] Although we strongly prefer our alternative, this is a debate that our nation needs to have, and we welcome the opportunity to weigh our ideas against all other options. The system will not be changed in the heat of a presidential campaign. The debate should begin now—before a few likely candidates for the next election build their stake in the current, corrupting system, and choose to block real reform. Regardless of what kind of campaign finance reforms get enacted, they should apply at the state and local levels, too.

Abuse of Campaign Finance in Judicial Elections

Judges are elected, not appointed on the basis of merit, in about two-thirds of the states. A fundamental question is whether potentially white-hot partisan elections are the proper method of choosing judges, who must decide dispassionately and impartially to protect the true and perceived fairness of our judicial system. Judges rightfully deserve praise for their public service and commitment to the pursuit of justice. But lawmakers put judges in a real bind when they enact laws that call for judicial elections. Under these circumstances, judges must raise contributions and seek the approval of voters. While such steps appear innocuous, they can lead to campaigns and interest groups engaging in mudslinging, and occasionally result in a judge who weighs decisions on a political balance. This scenario may sound all too familiar, as some judicial contests start to mirror the bickering and distortions that characterize many races for legislative and executive offices.

We believe that an appointment system would be far superior. Specifically, a nonpartisan commission should select judges based on merit. Such commissions, which are already in place in two-thirds of states,[112] recruit and recommend eligible nominees for judicial appointments. The commission's independence can be strengthened by dispersing power to appoint members of the commission across a variety of offices—the governor and legislators from both parties.

Appointment-based systems better serve their purpose when complemented by evaluation commissions. In 17 states, such commissions conduct thorough examinations of how judges perform during their terms. Criteria typically include understanding of relevant law, administrative prowess, and judicial temperament. As one study reports, "public confidence in judicial candidates and the judiciary as a whole is bolstered when voters receive such information through [judicial performance evaluation] programs." States can look to Arizona, whose Commission on Judicial Performance Review conducts routine assessments and even develops evaluation reports that the public can access, as a model.

Business has an important stake in the appearance and the reality of judicial impartiality. In one survey, seven out of 10 companies reported that a state's litigation climate is likely to impact important business decisions, such as where to locate. Among the eight states that received a top ranking for their business climates, only one held judicial contests. Robust market economies clearly depend on stable, even-handed legal environments—as do the tone of our society, and the prospects for the success of the capitalist system.

REFORM LOBBYING

As we noted in Chapter 1, the Constitution protects the right of citizens to free speech and to petition their government. Lobbying can fulfill a legitimate need for providing lawmakers and public administrators with useful perspectives about the workings of the private sector. But lobbying can be abused, and can become a tool for cronyism. In tandem with campaign finance reform, the lobbying system should be reformed to reduce special interest leverage over the legislative process. We should set stricter prohibitions on members of Congress and their staff from seeking employment in lobbying firms upon leaving Capitol Hill. For instance, we could lengthen to two years the so-called "cooling-off" period before a member who leaves the House may engage in any form of lobbying (this rule already applies in the Senate). The same restrictions could apply to employees of government agencies or regulatory authorities.

Also, we should ban any registered lobbyist, and any institution that hires registered lobbyists, from raising or soliciting contributions for federal candidates and officeholders. We should also ban registered lobbyists from serving as treasurers of Leadership PACs and other campaign fundraising organizations. We could also set lower-than-standard limits that a lobbyist might give personally for any campaign to a federal office.

Additionally, loopholes for cronyism need to be closed. We should place stricter limits on the number of political appointees that each successive administration can put in place. Although potential appointees will sometimes have backgrounds in the private business sector, limits on political appointees will reduce cronyism. Instead, we should strengthen our civil service. We should do this not only to counter cronyism, but also to improve government. This would entail ramping up talent and performance management capabilities to improve how we hire, develop, and reward top talent in the civil service, and how we remove poor performers.

Finally, we need to strengthen *enforcement* of laws and ethics rules that cover members of Congress, staff, and lobbyists. The committees with ethics responsibilities (the House Committee on Standards of Official Conduct, and the Senate Select Committee on Ethics) have not fulfilled their responsibilities. What may be needed, instead, is the establishment of a strong and independent enforcement authority to help Congress punish and deter ethical violations by lobbyists and members. A nonpartisan ethics enforcement authority, of a stature equivalent to the Congressional Budget Office, or perhaps within the Government Accountability Office, could be composed of distinguished former members of Congress and retired judges, insulated from political pressure. This independent ethics authority must have sufficient funding and professional, independent staff to fulfill all of its responsibilities. It would also need authority to initiate its own investigations, as well as the ability to receive complaints from members of Congress and the general public.

Fix Broken Redistricting Practices

Much of the partisan polarization and vanishing "middle" in Congress and in many state legislatures can be traced to redistricting practices that create safe districts. Individually, but often through implicit cooperation, both political parties abuse electoral redistricting practices to protect incumbents, which has the effect of radically reducing the number of competitive seats. Political parties are establishing electoral districts that effectively nullify the power of the vote of those who live in districts in which their candidates can never be elected. In effect, representatives in these districts are choosing their voters, not the other way around. This practice contributes to partisan polarization and the deterioration of the political process in Washington. It has led to the election of increasingly ideologically extreme representatives with little institutional loyalty, and an unprecedented degree of homogeneity within the two parties. It has made the party primary, with a traditionally low turnout dominated by activist voters, the election that counts. More-moderate voters are shut out of any meaningful role in the process. Appeals to the "base" drown out serious debate on broad issues of national concern. This has increased the importance of ideology in legislating and lobbying activities, contributing to gridlock; a divided, partisan Congress populated by few moderates; and a lack of comity and civility in Washington.

The manipulation of redistricting has advanced to such a stage that the United States must change its approach fundamentally. CED would welcome federal action. Failing that, we recommend that the states use their authority over the electoral process, delegated under the Constitution, to reform their own redistricting institutions. Legislation is needed to turn the responsibility for the decennial drawing of lines for House of Representative and state legislative offices to some form of nonpartisan commission whose mandate would be to create districts that are equal in population, compact, contiguous, and competitive (that is, approximately equally divided by party affiliation)—in that order of priority. A few states (including Arizona, California, and Ohio) have acted, although their efforts have been challenged. Progress to date should be protected, and other states should emulate those efforts.

FIX A FLAWED POLICYMAKING PROCESS

The influence of money and the pressures of partisanship have undermined essential rules and precedents of the legislative process. Citizens who watch the workings of the two Houses of the Congress see frequent flagrant abuse of rules and precedents that were accumulated and refined over decades for the express purpose of achieving fairness and deliberation. The universally accepted rules and procedures for the working of the legislative process—what had been known as the "regular order"—has been lost. In its place has grown a make-it-up-as-we-go system that allows congressional majorities to achieve Pyrrhic victories at the cost of consensus, comity, and therefore the nation's ability to address its crucial and contentious issues. These procedural abuses have a distinctly corrosive effect on the tradition of fair play in the public square, a tradition that binds Americans together. The same tactics have been practiced under leadership from both parties at different times, and a building cycle of alleged past abuse and following retribution has infected the Congress. Both parties are at fault.[113]

The mentality of the never-ending political campaign, in which legislators constantly fundraise rather than do their jobs, leads to last-minute legislation, including unrelated and unreviewed "riders." It precludes bipartisan cooperation for the fundamental tasks of program oversight and preparation of annual funding bills. Too often, hundreds of elected representatives must consider, at the last possible moment, huge bills that they cannot possibly grasp before voting, on a take-it-or-leave-it basis—where the failure to approve the must-pass bill is even worse than its extraneous content. Some members may be happy on one particular occasion that the small stowaway provision in the huge bill helps their constituents. But they must come to understand that in the future, they may find the equivalent rider odious. This is no way to govern, and it could eventually threaten the federal government's primacy, as well as its stability, and also budget control and fiscal responsibility. Those violations of the traditional rules must end and Congress should adopt a few additional rules to help it to function better.

Not every procedural problem can be solved with a rule, especially when the procedural problem besets an institution that writes—and therefore can change, or temporarily "waive"—its own rules. Some argue that individual rules could be protected by requirements that only a supermajority of votes can waive them. We are skeptical this would work. Even these requirements could be changed by majority vote. But also, the need for a supermajority to act can make the majority vulnerable to demands for special provisions by holdout members whose votes are needed. Business leaders should advocate reforms that could help rebuild the vital center in Washington, communicate that these reforms are needed urgently, and demonstrate a willingness to persist in pressing for change.

Reforms for Rebuilding the Vital Center

The following recommendations deserve business support to help rebuild the vital center.

- *The Congress should maintain its traditional "regular order."* The House should limit the use of closed rules (which function as "rules of engagement" for the consideration of a bill, and typically restrict the time allowed for debate and the numbers of amendments, sometimes effectively to zero through restrictions on the content or originator of one permitted amendment) to truly urgent pieces of legislation. This would allow for more deliberation and expression of a variety of views during debate. The House should also change its rules to specify that even under a closed rule, the minority should have the right to specify one amendment that it may offer. The regular order with adequate public notice should be used in scheduling House legislative and committee business. The rule specifying the minimum layover time from publication to voting for bills should be actualized by conducting such essential business as annual appropriations for federal agencies on a timely basis, so that potential gross damage to the public well-being does not require that the rule be waived.

- *The House and the Senate promptly should appoint members to conference committees, including members from the minority party.* Chief among these appointments should be those responsible for drafting the legislation. Conference committees should then meet on a bipartisan, open basis to debate and vote on the issues in the respective bills.

- *Congress (especially the House) should change its schedule to comprise at least two-week periods of Monday-through-Friday sessions, with weeks off in between to allow time in their home districts.* Such a schedule would allow more time for oversight and substantive hearings. It would also bring the members together much more than the current schedule. With such acquaintance might well come better understanding of the perspectives of others, and greater attempts to achieve consensus. This could be enforced by a rule that would prohibit the House or the Senate from adjourning unless it had held a minimum number of such periods.

- *The House should use self-executing rules, which change bills passed by committees of jurisdiction before they go to the House floor, sparingly.* Self-executing rules should be used only in instances of true emergencies or where revisions of bills are purely in the nature of technical correction rather than substantive alteration.

- *Senate holds should be cut back to their former purpose of allowing senators to exercise their judgment on nominations from their states, only.* The frequency and duration of filibusters in recent years, widely cited in the press, have been excessive. However, filibusters may be more symptoms of Congress failing to seek bipartisan consensus and to include the broad ideological center, rather than causes of the true problem.

- *The concept of "scope" in conference should be restored, such that new provisions (those included in neither the House nor the Senate bill) would not be in order in conference reports.* All decisions in conference committees should be made by the members, not the staff, and should be made with the awareness of all the members.

- *Congress should rededicate itself to timely appropriations.* Delays and uncertainty in funding waste taxpayer dollars, and render government less effective and efficient. Appropriations bills should be debated individually and in the open, not in omnibus continuing appropriations passed in the dead of night.

- *Congress should reenact budget disciplines—spending caps for annual appropriations, and pay-as-you-go requirements for entitlement spending and taxes—that worked effectively in the 1990s.* Mere deficit neutrality in entitlements and taxes will not be enough to correct the rising deficits that are likely in the coming years.

- *Congress should fulfill its obligation to prepare an annual budget—not a political wish list or an economic prayer, but rather a serious plan for the allocation of the public's scarce tax dollars that can be implemented in law.* And the Congress, on a bipartisan basis, should implement that plan with individual, on-time appropriations bills that are shaped through a conscientious oversight process. The time that such oversight requires could be recovered from the hours now spent seeking campaign contributions.

The vital center must be rebuilt so that Washington can get back to constructive work. The recommendations for reform numerated here are pragmatic, nonpartisan suggestions aimed at repairing processes and practices that are interfering with good government, impairing our society, and stifling our economy. Taking action on all of these critical issues—from reducing the influence of money in politics to following once again civil rules of procedure in the House of Representatives—is long overdue. The business community must step up to raise the level of awareness of every citizen to the consequences of poor government performance—and the pragmatic steps we can take to improve it. Rebuilding trust in the institutions of government will make it possible for America's elected policymakers to once again address the country's crucial economic issues—and make capitalism sustainable by making it work for all our people.

6

A Prescription for Fiscal Health

ONE OF THE MOST CRITICAL ISSUES that Congress and the President have failed to resolve—or even address—is the nation's fiscal *ill* health. This failure poses a threat to the stability of the entire economy. After many years of running high budget deficits and borrowing to cover outlays, the nation's debt burden has grown to dangerously high levels. The most important measure of our federal budget problem is the size of our debt burden as a share of the nation's total economy, which is to say, our public debt as a percentage of our gross domestic product (GDP). To be clear, it is not necessarily irresponsible for the government to run a budget deficit in any particular year, thereby incurring debt.[114] What is dangerous is the enormity of the nation's debt load, and the risk that continued deficits can feed upon themselves, fueling ever-growing debt to still more dangerous levels.

The United States has enormous financial strength. It is the largest economy in the world, with high standards of living. Our Treasury's bills, notes, and bonds are by reputation a gilt-edged store of value, and are held as reserves by governments, financial institutions and other businesses, and individuals all around the world. Comparisons of our nation to highly challenged governments and economies elsewhere are remote. But our recent fiscal behavior has put all of that advantage to unnecessary and imprudent risk. Continuing that behavior, even if the worst is avoided, will erode American prosperity—trading current consumption for a lower standard of living for all future generations, and risking our position of world economic leadership. Dollars spent to service the public debt cannot finance either capacity-increasing private investment in plant and equipment, or productivity-increasing public investment in education, research, or infrastructure.

And that is if the worst is avoided. Yes, the U.S. fiscal state does not bear immediate comparison to that of highly troubled nations elsewhere. But on its current path our debt burden is precariously close to the entry point of a vicious cycle of debt service obligations feeding upon themselves. History provides no useful lessons in what would happen if the world's leading economy, the issuer of the world's financial reserve currency, were to find itself engulfed by runaway debt. But clearly, it would be unforgivably irresponsible to provide that history lesson to today's world, and to America's future. It would truly threaten the sustainability of our capitalist system.

Consider the potential fallout, which can create a vicious, ever-worsening cycle.

Most fundamentally, a rising public debt begets rising interest obligations. Furthermore, interest rates may rise for multiple reasons, including straightforward cyclical domestic economic factors—accelerating economic growth that increases the demand for credit, or fears of rising domestic inflation. Similarly, a falling dollar can increase the interest rates needed to attract foreign credit (and also the prospects for inflation, by increasing the prices of imports). Or interest rates can increase because of an increase in the perceived risk of the Treasury's promise to service and to repay the debt—such as through an official ratings downgrade, or political mishandling of the need to increase our statutory debt limit, or from simple recognition of the increased debt burden itself. And finally, interest rates can rise because of factors beyond our borders (and therefore potentially beyond our control), such as foreign economic or financial crises, or worsening global perceptions of the United States (including perceived dissipation of our own sovereignty because of our rising debt).

FIGURE 6.1   Foreign and Domestic Purchases of U.S. Public Debt, Billions of Dollars, March 2001–December 2015

Source: Treasury Bulletin, June 2016, data for December 2015 (https://www.fiscal.treasury.gov/fsreports/rpt/treasBulletin/current.htm).

If and when those forces build, they reinforce one another, and raise the Treasury's cost of servicing the public debt with interest payments. Any failure to meet those interest obligations would have extreme consequences, including an inability to borrow further or the imposition of much higher interest rates on new or even existing debt, which could send the value of the currency into a plunge and interest rates and inflation soaring, thereby diminishing standards of living. Today, the federal government is highly dependent on borrowed money—almost two-thirds of it from other nations (see Figure 6.1, "Foreign and Domestic Purchases of U.S. Public Debt")—and maintaining its ability to borrow is essential to meeting all of its financial obligations. If access to the credit markets should be interrupted, the government would be forced to respond with immediate tax increases and spending cuts, which would weigh heavily on all of those who depend on government for business, employment, or benefits, and would surely degrade fundamental public services ranging from national security to food safety. In the meantime, the value of Treasury securities would fall. Financial institutions in the United States and globally rely upon Treasury securities as reserves and collateral, and a fall in their value would disrupt financial markets and send households and businesses into insolvency. The result would be utter economic chaos—far worse than the recent financial crisis whose impact was so painful.

Debt must be serviced; the larger the debt, the larger the amount of debt service; and the larger the amount of debt service, the greater the risk to the lender that adverse developments will render that debt-service obligation difficult or even impossible to meet. The U.S. debt burden is both rising and already too high. To cite a reasonable standard by which to judge, the framers of the Maastricht Treaty of 1992 for the creation of the European Monetary Union (the EMU, using the euro as its currency) set 60 percent of a nation's GDP as the maximum tolerable debt burden for its members. All nations that have since aspired to use the euro as their currency have pledged to maintain their public debt burdens below that 60 percent level. Although any such specific numeric ceiling is somewhat arbitrary, the reason for a limit as a proportion of the total economy is fairly clear.

Consider U.S. public debt in historical perspective. The nation accumulated the heaviest debt burden in its history, now estimated at 106.1 percent of our GDP, at the end of World War II. (See Figure 6.2, "Actual and Projected U.S. Public Debt").[115] With the highly favorable economic and budgetary conditions at the end of the war—healthy consumer balance sheets, pent-up demand after wartime rationing and shortages, a burgeoning labor force from the return of the troops, the peaceful re-direction of newly developed wartime technology, and the substantial budgetary savings from the winding down of the war effort—the debt burden as a percentage of the GDP plunged from that 1946 peak of 106.1 percent to between 27.1 percent and 23.1 percent from 1971 through 1981. The debt almost doubled to 47.8 percent in 1993, fell by more than a third to 31.4 percent in 2001, and then rose again to a range of 34.5 percent to 35.2 percent from 2003 to 2007.

Even in 2007, budget forecasters considered the outlook dire. At the time, the nonpartisan Congressional Budget Office projected figures indicating that the then-current budget policy would send the

FIGURE 6.2   Actual and Projected U.S. Public Debt, 1946–2026

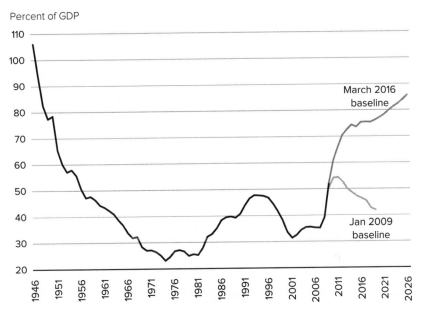

Percent of GDP

Source: Congressional Budget Office, Budget and Economic Data, 10-Year Budget Projections, March 2016 and January 2009 (https://www.cbo.gov/about/products/budget_economic_data#2).

debt-to-GDP ratio to its danger level of 60 percent by 2022. But then the financial crisis hit, and the lurking problem attacked with unexpected speed, exacerbated by stimulus spending without subsequent reform. The debt burden leapt to 60.9 percent in 2010, and has risen further to an estimated 73.6 percent at the end of fiscal 2015. (See Figure 6.3, "Deterioration of U.S. Public Debt Outlook"). It appears that this upward trend will continue unabated. In a report released in July of 2016, the CBO projected that the U.S. debt-to-GDP ratio would rise continuously to 141 percent by 2046 if tax and spending policies are not changed. The primary driver of this growth is spending on Medicare and Social Security, which is increasing due to the aging of the population and higher medical costs.

Though the U.S. public debt burden already significantly exceeds the 60 percent warning signal, for now, the fiscal weakness of the rest of

FIGURE 6.3   Deterioration of U.S. Public Debt Outlook, December 2007–Present

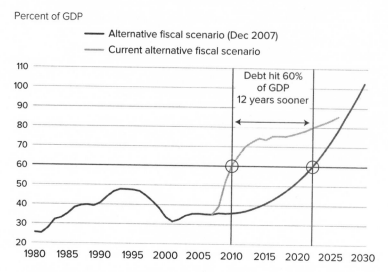

Source: Congressional Budget Office, March 2016 report *Updated Budget Projections: 2016 to 2026*, Figure 2 (https://www.cbo.gov/about/products/budget_economic_data); CBO, Projected long-term spending and revenues—December 2007, Figures 1–2 (https://www.cbo.gov/publication/42468).

the world has rendered our debt problem benign to investors. As other, smaller developed nations have accumulated their own substantial budget deficits, the U.S. fiscal situation, with a longer track record, the dollar's status as the world's reserve currency, and the Treasury's widely traded securities, has looked less troubling by comparison. Given the choice of nations in which to park their money, investors—including foreign governments—have continued to choose the United States. This has helped to stabilize U.S. financial markets and put downward pressure on interest rates. But markets may not forebear reaction for long. If the U.S. debt burden, already at a worrisome level, continues to grow (including potential contagion from troubled state government budgets), an adverse reaction in the financial markets will eventually become all but certain.[116]

Investors could decide to retreat from reliance on Treasury securities at any time. That retreat could be restrained, with investors demanding somewhat higher interest rates. If past patterns hold, those higher interest rates will be passed on to business and consumer borrowers through relatively constant "yield spreads" above the benchmark of Treasury securities for corporate bonds, residential mortgages, and all other species of credit instruments. Those higher interest rates would discourage investment and therefore would inhibit future productivity, economic growth, and living standards. The consequent increase in the federal government's debt-service costs would make it harder for government to finance any and all public services. Alternatively, the debt could cause a knee-jerk "rush for the exits" reaction, which could be far more serious.

On the other hand, some economists disagree, believing debt concerns to be overblown. Most of these counter-arguments boil down to the five reasoned objections described next.

Objection 1: *Economic growth is slow, and productivity growth is slow. The United States should not tighten budgetary policy during times of such slow growth.*

Although the unemployment rate already is low, some economists argue that fiscal authorities can make the economy grow faster by running large budget deficits, and that the economy still has substantial headroom to expand without inflation. To make this case, they also argue that many workers who exited the labor force during the financial crisis have not yet returned.

But all of that is most likely not the case. The unemployment rate is down more than five full percentage points from October 2009, when it peaked at 10 percent, falling to below 5 percent during 2016; and real wages are beginning to grow. With wages already rising, future employment growth without inflation will require a substantial number of re-entries of current discouraged workers, as well as upgrading of part-time workers and workers not fully utilizing their skills. This is because the unemployment rate does not have much more room to fall, and the working-age population is growing slowly. This may be too optimistic. The only alternatives are a significant acceleration of productivity growth (such as through automation), or a rapid acceleration of immigration to expand the labor force. Large budget deficits won't likely result in faster productivity growth in the short run because firms already are seeking productivity growth to increase their own profits. In the longer run, large budget deficits—even if a serious financial crisis is avoided—will inhibit productivity growth, because they crowd out private-sector investment. This creates a vicious cycle because slower economic growth aggravates the budget problem. A rapid growth of immigration would be difficult to target closely to skills in shortage.

Put another way, if the U.S. economy had high unemployment and slow growth, there could be a strong argument to allow the federal budget deficit to rise.[117] But with unemployment low and with the economy growing slowly anyway, it is far from clear that larger budget deficits will accelerate growth. More spending merely will drive employers to bid against each other for the same labor and capital goods, leading to higher inflation, not more growth. What is needed is more innovation and productivity growth—and these cannot be bought with bigger deficits. Large deficits can be a tool for unique situations, but there is no excuse for running large deficits perpetually, regardless of the macroeconomic circumstances.

Objection 2: If the financial markets had any fear of the nation's ability to manage its debt, interest rates would be high and rising. Instead, interest rates are on the floor. This is clear evidence that we are nowhere near a debt crisis. In fact, "expert" forecasts of impending interest rate increases have been put off several times. If interest rates remain low, there is no problem.

True: A debt crisis will most likely manifest itself early on through a sharp rise in interest rates. The fundamental reason interest rates are low is that economic growth remains sluggish in the wake of the financial crisis, not just in the United States but all around the world. The Federal Reserve's extraordinary response to the economic weakness has held interest rates lower still. The willingness of foreigners to invest in the "safe haven" of the United States, given even worse prospects in the rest of the world, adds more downward pressure on U.S. interest rates.

But no one should assume that interest rates will remain low forever. Our concern about the nation's fiscal health is not the certainty of some future calamity, but the excessive and growing risk to which greater debt subjects the nation. Once market participants come to believe that interest rates will rise, they will act to make that happen. Like people who begin to smell smoke in a crowded theater, they will not walk slowly to the exits; they will run to protect the principal of their investments from the falling value of bonds when interest rates rise. The likelihood of such a panic reaction is an important reason the nation should steer clear of such risks.

Taking current forecasts of low future interest rates as a free pass to pile up debt is like a household maxing out a credit line on temporary "teaser" rates. Even those who make this low-rate argument hope for a full and robust economic recovery. When that recovery occurs, interest rates will rise. If the nation piles up debt in the interim, we could someday find ourselves with an unsustainable debt load and only impossible choices facing us. It would be irresponsible to lead ourselves blithely down that blind alley.

Objection 3: The ratio of the public debt to the GDP has stabilized. The problem has been solved. Move along, folks—there's nothing to see here.

The logic behind this objection is as follows: an important dashboard indicator of the fiscal state of the nation is the ratio of the debt to the GDP. The debt-to-GDP ratio has been on a roller-coaster ride over the last five decades, but near-term projections suggest a brief interval of stability.[118] The budget deficit peaked at $1.413 trillion in 2009, in the teeth of the crisis, but then fell to $438 billion in 2015. The debt-to-GDP ratio declined from 74.4 percent in 2014 to 73.6 percent in 2015. Problem solved, some would say.

It isn't—for two reasons. First, the projected slowdown of the debt burden is only temporary. By CBO's baseline, the debt-to-GDP ratio has begun to climb again, and will rise to 85.5 percent by 2026, the end of the current ten-year projection window.

Second, even this troubling CBO baseline is inherently optimistic. It assumes that forthcoming budget policy will follow the current law. Current law includes rigorous—some would say unrealistic—future spending cuts, known as the "sequester." The "sequester" has been loosened twice—once for two years (fiscal years 2014–15) in a last-minute budget deal in 2013, and again for the current two following budgeting years (2016–17) in another budget deal that was brokered in October, 2015. And these two deals clearly portend more concessions to come in future years. Quite plainly, the Congress cannot write and enact appropriations bills at the low post-sequester levels. Even many small-government advocates in the Congress want more spending on the programs that benefit their districts than can be accommodated within the current-law sequester levels. And allowance for only the sequester's bare-bones spending levels in an already high-deficit budget leaves no room for contingencies.

Furthermore, the baseline assumes future tax increases, in the form of expirations of so-called "extender" temporary tax cuts, which are highly unlikely to occur. Without the continuation of the sequester spending cuts and the expiration of the extender tax cuts, the debt burden would increase much faster than the official baseline. Elimination of the sequester spending cuts, plus continuation of all of the extender tax cuts, plus the resulting debt-service costs, would increase the debt accumulated by 2026 by more than $2.5 trillion—or more than 9 percentage points of 2026 GDP. This would push the debt-to-GDP ratio in 2026 to over 95 percent. By that time, whether the budget achieves baseline projections or not, the debt will have grown so large that it, plus interest rates rising from today's rock-bottom levels, will have rendered the budget far more vulnerable to any unfavorable developments.

Objection 4: The budget deficit and the debt have declined more than projected during the last few years, now that the worst of the financial crisis is behind us. It would be worth betting that these fortunate budget outlook revisions will continue. Why accept the pain of budget consolidation with spending cuts and tax increases when the problem might solve itself?

That's a bad bet. Merely hoping for budget outcomes better than forecast is imprudent at best; at worst it's an irresponsibly high-stakes gamble, with the well-being of future generations as the ante. The economy and the budget might continue to outperform projections; but they could just as likely underperform them. If the optimistic view proves to be wrong the consequences could be catastrophic. The markets could balk even at the budget baseline, which would be the worst non-wartime debt performance in U.S. history. It's impossible to predict whether the financial markets will perceive the outcome of any such risky policy decision to be excessive debt. But once the markets react, it will already be too late. The damage could be done in weeks, or days, or even hours; after the scars of the financial crisis, the damage could be irreversible. This is just too much risk for prudent stewards of the nation's future to incur.

Objection 5: We can live indefinitely with public debt equal to 75 percent of the GDP. It isn't so bad. In fact, after World War II, the debt was more than 106 percent of the GDP, and we grew out of that. We can do it again.

While the rate of change of the debt burden (the public debt expressed as a percentage of the GDP) is one dashboard indicator of the fiscal health of the federal government, the *level* of the debt burden is another. If the nation had entered the 2008 recession with a very low debt burden, the budget deficits that followed would have been less worrisome. But the debt burden—fueled by reduced tax revenues and high safety net outlays triggered by the recession, and adverse changes in public policy— has more than doubled since the beginning of the financial crisis, and should any other substantial contingency arise today, the nation will be even more vulnerable to a currency crisis and spiking interest rates and inflation, and more inhibited in its ability to respond.

Consider the differences between the post-war U.S. economy, and today's U.S. economy. In 1946—with the wisdom of hindsight and the benefit of subsequent economic thought—the U.S. economy was uniquely poised for growth. The civilian labor force swelled with the returning troops. The civilian industrial base multiplied itself as investors converted military production facilities to civilian use, and wartime technologies to civilian goods. Much of the rest of the developed world was devastated by war, while the United States, unscathed, could produce and export goods for rebuilding those countries. And perhaps most important, the U.S. household population had healthy, even buoyant balance sheets, because of wartime years of full employment coupled with suppressed spending because of shortages and rationing. The national budget, in essence, capitalized on all of this instant prosperity. Plus there was immediate and substantial deficit reduction from the end of the war effort; defense spending fell from 36.6 percent of GDP in 1945 to 5.4 percent in 1947, and 3.5 percent in 1948. The result was an immediate drop in federal government spending, to complement the sharp increase in the civilian portion of the GDP.

The situation today is the diametric opposite. Workforce growth has slowed to a near-standstill because of the aging of the baby-boom generation (whose oldest members, born in 1946, are already age 71 in 2017, and whose youngest, born in 1964, will be 55 years old in just 2019). It is not the U.S. industrial base that is mushrooming, but rather the competitive productive capacity of nations in the industrialized and the developing worlds. The U.S. household sector has a balance sheet that's been depleted since the housing bubble burst, while the stock-market crash of the financial crisis forced many households, especially retirees, to dissipate much of their savings. What's more, defense spending is less than 3.5 percent of GDP, and thus reducing it cannot possibly provide the magnitude of savings than it did after World War II.

In 1946 the U.S. budget was on a course for decades of steady and sometimes rapid improvement. Today, in contrast, the budget faces enormous obstacles to progress. This is not to belittle the importance of economic growth as a factor for reducing deficits and debt. Sustained faster growth could contribute importantly, while sustained slower growth than now anticipated could make the problem virtually unmanageable.[119] The nation surely should invest for future growth—through a more highly skilled workforce, better infrastructure, and research—and create a better economic environment through reformed health care and tax systems. But government has a track record of assuming robust increases in growth from such initiatives, and then spending the full amount of the assumed budgetary bonus up front, even before the growth benefits materialize—and in most instances, the assumed growth was overstated and proved elusive. The same mistake can't be made again.

Complacency is a mistake, too. If policymakers decide that they can live with a debt as large as 75 percent of our GDP, and develop no plan to reduce that debt burden when the economy is growing and the news is good, then at some point in the future, bad news is sure to follow. The debt will quickly get out of hand, sooner or later, inevitably, when interest rates rise, other spending increases, or revenues fall, as soon as something goes wrong. The 2016 presidential election campaign has failed to address this issue.

This Way Down—To a Debt Crisis

What could go wrong for the sovereign government of the world's largest economy? Sadly, recent history provides numerous examples, which we will describe in the following section.[120]

National security emergencies. The United States continues to face serious national security challenges. The cost of fighting wars in the Middle East has amounted to multiple trillions of dollars as of 2016 (including likely future obligations).[121] The United States could find itself faced with another substantial national security challenge—and if so, current debt levels could seriously constrain U.S. options. Undertaking military action, on the magnitude of the Gulf War, could raise such doubts about the ability and willingness to service the country's public debt that it would trigger instability in the financial markets. Not responding to a threat because of our debt load might set in motion geo-political consequences that would be equally harmful.

Natural disasters. Some members of Congress argue that the national response costs to earthquakes, extreme weather events, or contagious disease outbreaks should be offset by cuts in other spending, because of the potential consequences for the budget. Delays in responding to emergency situations because of the fiscal implications would raise questions about the nation's financial stability and its status as a world leader.

Domestic economic events. The United States added trillions of dollars to the public debt over three fiscal years in the wake of the last financial crisis—what about the next one? If the events of 2008 were to be reprised today, with no plan in place to undo the buildup of debt, it would take that debt burden to unprecedented and dangerous levels.

Consider also that circumstances could arise under which the federal government would need to step in and make financial commitments to resolve failing financial institutions before their collapse would cascade into even more widespread failures. Financial markets can be calmed more easily when it is clear that a lender of last resort can make such commitments. If the financial markets were to question the ability of the federal government to act because its debt already was excessive and growing, it could unleash panic.[122]

There also could be serious financial fallout from a more straightforward economic downturn. Today, a downturn caused by excess inventories easily could add hundreds of billions of dollars to the debt. The rapid rise of the debt caused by a deep recession could pose a "Catch-22" dilemma: it could demand fiscal stimulus to arrest the downturn, while at the same time frightening off the lenders who would be called upon to finance the resulting budget deficits.

Global economic events. Financial events in other countries also pose threats to the United States. In today's world, U.S. financial institutions are reliant upon institutions in other nations to make good on their commitments. Failures of institutions abroad could weaken U.S. financial institutions to the point where the federal government must step in and provide liquidity domestically. If the ability of the United States to provide such support were subject to question—because of an excessive buildup of public debt—it could make the eruption of a financial crisis more likely.

Political miscalculation. Perhaps the greatest threat to U.S. financial stability comes from a failure to increase the debt limit and thereby to allow the Treasury to borrow the cash it needs to fulfill its obligations. An appropriations standoff (a "government shutdown") would have less direct impact on the country's financial standing, although it would detract from public respect for the nation and thereby have an indirect impact. Given that debt limit expirations sometimes are scheduled to occur at the same time as appropriations deadlines, however, even seemingly unrelated appropriations fights can aggravate disputes over raising the debt limit.

In October and November of 2013, as the Treasury approached the date at which it had announced that it would run out of cash and borrowing authority to pay the federal government's bills, there were identifiable impacts on the interest rates that investors would accept on the Treasury securities that would have been affected, potentially costing the Treasury substantial sums in additional debt service. (See Figure 6.4, "Secondary Market Yields on Treasury Bills Maturing in Late October through Mid-November 2013 (in Basis Points)).[123] Partisans squabble over whether a cash-short Treasury could "prioritize" and avoid falling behind on interest payments or redemption of maturing securities by delaying the payment of other obligations. However, a Treasury that was picking coins out of the figurative sofa to avoid a formal default easily could arouse a reaction in the financial markets to the full adverse effect of a default by the strictest definition. The markets rely on Treasury securities as fully secure; any manipulation to skirt narrowly defined

FIGURE 6.4   Secondary Market Yields on Treasury Bills Maturing in Late
October through Mid-November 2013 (in basis points)

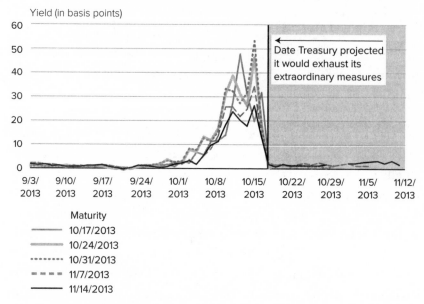

Source: Presented in U.S. Government Accountability Office, GAO-15-476, *Debt Limit: Market Responses to Recent Impasses Underscores Need to Consider Alternative Approaches*, July 2015, Figure 2, page 16.

default could harm the nation's financial status even if it succeeded, and certainly if it failed.

Market sentiment. Financial markets run on psychology and can turn on the skimpiest of evidence. The Dow Jones Industrial Average on "Black Monday," October 19, 1987, lost almost 23 percent of its value. Needless to say, there was no development on the weekend preceding Black Monday that would have indicated that the U.S. corporate sector was suddenly worth 23 percent less than it had been at the close of the trading day on the preceding Friday. But should serious questions be raised about the reliability of the United States as a debtor, that realization easily could have such a magnitude of impact on markets, and on the value of Treasury securities.

The Prescription

Given the nation's recent accumulation of public debt, and the unwillingness of elected policymakers to contemplate any remedy, the risk of a serious financial and economic dislocation is far greater than prudent public stewardship would allow. This is potentially an existential issue for American capitalism. Business leaders should encourage responsible policymakers to set aside their partisan differences and begin at once to build both mutual trust and a plan to address the fiscal problem.

Restoring the nation's fiscal health will require major and broadly based changes in public policy. The debt has grown so large that no single remedy—no "silver bullet"—will suffice. Principled compromise is essential. Therefore, efforts to reduce the national debt and rein in deficits must be bipartisan. Hence the challenge. Most critically, policymakers need to reform health care entitlement programs, especially Medicare, as they are at the heart of the country's long-term debt crisis. But touching only health care will not suffice. Policymakers also must restrain discretionary spending, reform corporate and individual taxes, and fix Social Security, among other necessary steps—and all of these are anathema to one side or another in a divided Washington.

Hope for concrete progress on all these issues glimmered briefly in Washington just a few years ago. In 2010, the Bipartisan Policy Center (BPC) convened a Debt Reduction Task Force (DRTF) of 19 former elected officials and experienced citizens with diverse backgrounds from across the political spectrum. The task force's recommendations—also referred to as the Domenici-Rivlin plan, after its two co-chairs, former Senate Budget Committee Chair Pete Domenici (R-NM) and former CBO and OMB Director Alice Rivlin—raised awareness of the extent of America's fiscal problems, and the need for an integrated set of reforms to improve the nation's fiscal health. CED contributed extensively to this effort, and the proposed reforms were endorsed by CED.[124]

(Similar proposals were put forward by the National Commission on Fiscal Responsibility and Reform, the "Simpson-Bowles Commission," named after co-chairs former Senator Alan Simpson, Republican of Idaho, and former White House Chief of Staff Erskine Bowles.)

Congress passed a few components of these proposals into law—most notably the caps on annually appropriated spending contained in the Budget Control Act of 2011, which included reductions in defense and non-defense discretionary spending. But far more needs to be done to reach a compromise that calls on both political parties to make tough choices. Business leaders can prepare a sensible path forward by encouraging policymakers to set aside their partisan differences and develop a plan that will address the fiscal problem in a comprehensive way. The concrete policy steps to do so follow.

Reform Medicare

Medicare is charged to give seniors access to quality, affordable care. Over recent years, the affordability of Medicare for the federal government gravely has eroded. Without real reform to make Medicare fiscally sustainable, the access and quality for seniors will be impossible to maintain. Medicare is enormously important to millions of U.S. seniors. They have health care coverage, despite the potentially enormous costs that can beset any older person, solely because of Medicare's protections earned through enrollees' contributions during their working years.

We can give Medicare enrollees better care. And we can give them better choices that provide the kinds of plans that different seniors want. Preferences differ, and one size does not fit all. Perhaps most importantly, we can give today's working population a sustainable Medicare program that they can count upon for their retirement years. That would be a key part of making capitalism sustainable. This threat to Medicare forces us to seek higher quality care at lower costs. That threat has two dimensions: the rising cost of care for each senior, and the rising number of seniors in the program.

The rising cost of delivering health care on a per-person basis is a drag on every budget in the nation. Businesses trying to maintain a constant level of coverage for their employees and their families have faced rising costs that have cramped investments in innovation and new, near-term productive capacity. These rising costs also have depressed wage gains and other forms of employee compensation, such as pension contributions. Households have had their spendable incomes pinched by rising premium payments, higher co-pay costs and deductibles, cutbacks in coverage, and ultimately by reduced growth of cash take-home pay.

Medicare also has reeled from rising health care costs, but its challenges are even greater than those faced by businesses and households, or by private health insurers. The demographic realities of the American population drive a worsening picture ahead, as the oversized baby boom generation continues to age and retire. Care for the elderly is more heavily a public cost, and Medicare's costs have been growing more rapidly than the nation's collective income—out of which those costs must

FIGURE 6.5   Medicare and Other Health Care Programs as Sources of Non-Interest Spending Growth

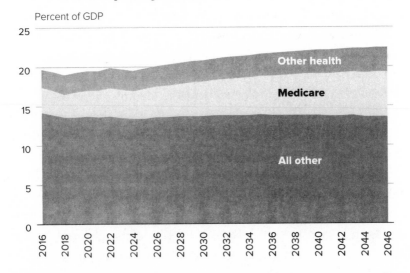

Source: Authors' calculation based on Congressional Budget Office, *The 2016 Long-Term Budget Outlook*, July 12, 2016, https://www.cbo.gov/about/products/budget_economic_data#1.

be paid. In fact, because of these two forces—rising health care costs per beneficiary, and the rising number of beneficiaries—Medicare is the single most powerful driver behind the projected future growth of the public debt. The Congressional Budget Office (CBO) estimates that by 2046, taking account of all savings claimed by the Affordable Care Act and all of the recent good news regarding slower-than-anticipated growth in health care costs, spending on Medicare will have increased by 2.5 percent of GDP, while other federal health care spending will have increased by another 0.8 percent of GDP. But taken together, all other components of non-interest spending are projected on net to *reduce* the deficit by 0.6 percent of GDP.[125] This means the entire increase in interest on the debt, and all of the increase in debt and deficits, will be due to the increase in Medicare plus other health care spending.[126] (See Figure 6.5, "Medicare and Other Health Care Programs as Sources of Non-Interest Spending Growth.")

Seniors need quality health care. The current Medicare model clearly isn't sustainable, and cannot provide that quality care, given the uncontrollable costs. So what's to be done? Making large cuts in physician reimbursements, advocated by some, is not the answer, as that only incentivizes physicians to drop patients with Medicare, or to seek to recover those fee cuts from beneficiaries themselves or by shifting them to the private sector. Medicare rapidly would become a "second-tier" health care system. Although current law empowers a national Independent Payment Advisory Board (IPAB) to identify and mandate cost-saving measures for Medicare, the remote IPAB's recommendations are unlikely to marry quality and savings—though they could well interfere with the hands-on relationship between doctors and patients.

A better alternative is to unleash market forces to drive down Medicare's program cost while improving the quality of care received by beneficiaries in the system. (Market-driven solutions can drive health care costs down across the board. See the sidebar to this chapter, "Putting Consumer Choice into Health Care.") Allowing many private plans to compete to provide health care coverage packages to the nation's senior

TABLE 6.1   **Modernizing Medicare through Medicare Advantage**

RECOMMENDATION	EFFECT
1a. Eliminate Medicare Advantage (MA) price "benchmark" based on traditional Medicare fee-for-service cost.	Remove influence of inflation-prone, inefficient fee-for-service medicine on Medicare costs.
1b. Require MA plans to submit prices competitively, unconstrained by Medicare "benchmark." Allow plans to bid as low as their efficiency allows. Plans may offer variations with greater coverages and services at higher premium prices if they so choose.	Give plans the incentive to achieve efficiencies while maintaining quality, enabling them to bid lower to attract customers.
1c. Provide enrollees with a nonrefundable, single-purpose, advanceable credit that they can use to buy the lowest or the second-lowest-price plan (either MA or traditional Medicare) at no out-of-pocket cost. Allow enrollees to purchase more-expensive plans by paying the incremental cost above the second-lowest-price plans. (Enrollees pay an equivalent of the current-law Part B and Part D premiums subject to changes specified below.)	Enrollees choose plans based on their own preferences, quality, and price. Plans are driven by competition to achieve efficiencies to satisfy consumers, leading to pressure for continuous improvement and innovation.
2a. Increase the income conditioning of enrollee Part B and Part D premiums.	Upper-income beneficiaries pay higher premiums. Net program cost and the federal budget deficit and public debt are reduced accordingly.
2b. Temporarily reduce Part B premiums for current low-income beneficiaries who face increased costs if they choose to continue to use traditional Medicare. (New enrollees pay current-law Part B premiums, as modified above. Current enrollees who switch to lower-cost MA plans keep part of the savings.)	Allow low-income enrollees who have ongoing programs of care and relationships with current Medicare providers to continue that care with little or no out-of-pocket cost. Allow new low-income enrollees to obtain coverage at no out-of-pocket cost if they choose the low-priced plans but without any reduction in their current Part B and Part D premium-equivalents.
3. Risk-adjust plan premium revenue.	Reward plans that take on sick patients; discourage plans from seeking out only healthy patients.
4. Identify a minimum threshold for availability of MA plans in rural areas. Until MA plans are generally available and accepted by providers, allow beneficiaries to enroll in traditional Medicare at no additional out-of-pocket cost.	Protect rural enrollees who do not have access to true MA options from premium increases for traditional Medicare.

citizens would do far more to identify and drive health care system cost savings than a single independent and remote board such as the IPAB.[127] Market forces could be unleashed if individual Medicare beneficiaries could choose on the basis of quality and price among private plans and the traditional Medicare system, competing on a level playing field.

The current Medicare Advantage (MA) program could be used as the foundation for a market-based reform of Medicare. MA is a voluntary private alternative to traditional fee-for-service (FFS) Medicare. Over the past 24 years, voluntary enrollment in private-plan MA has grown from 6 percent to 31 percent of all Medicare enrollees.[128] Even more notably, after MA cuts in the Affordable Care Act of 2010 were projected to reduce MA enrollment, it instead increased sharply. Today's MA plans are required to offer lower co-pays and deductibles than traditional Medicare, and usually do so for the same (or effectively a lower) cost. The success of MA—along with the similar success of the Medicare Part D prescription drug program—shows both that private insurance plans bidding competitively can deliver health care that people want, and that seniors can make good choices among alternative private plans.

The Medicare Program pays privately delivered Medicare Advantage "insurance" premiums, in full or in part, according to a formula (the "benchmark") based on the cost of traditional fee-for-service Medicare in the beneficiary's geographic area. There are some MA plans that are more expensive than the formula-based payment from Medicare, and if an enrollee wants such a plan, he or she is responsible for paying the difference.

MA plans commonly are "managed care" offerings, structured as integrated delivery systems (IDSs), or alternatively as something like preferred provider organizations (PPOs) that use restricted networks of cooperating but independent physicians. These plans generally serve specific geographic areas. On average, beneficiaries can choose from among 18 plans in their area as alternatives to traditional fee-for-service Medicare.

Today, Medicare Advantage plans operate by offering a base bid to cover core hospital and physician health care services (Medicare Parts A and B) and usually also prescription drugs (Part D—always with reduced enrollee cost sharing). If the plan believes it can achieve efficiencies, such that it could underbid the benchmark price in its region, it can't lower premiums and charge enrollees less. Rather, the plan is limited to use 50–70 percent of the savings (depending on the plan's "star" quality rating) to offer some indirect form of savings to the enrollee, through further reduction in enrollee co-pays or deductibles, or additional coverage benefits (such as free eyeglasses or health club memberships), in a package that might prove attractive to enrollees (and therefore more competitive among alternative plans). The remaining 30–50 percent of the savings must go to the federal Treasury.

But this does little to motivate beneficiaries to seek out more-efficient plans, and not enough to motivate plans to pursue operating efficiencies. The incentive is misdirected. Instead of sharing cost efficiency savings with the enrollees and the federal government, for example, the current system implicitly encourages plans to keep all of the savings, or to spend all of the money on advertising and marketing.

To truly drive competition, innovation, and higher quality at lower cost, a simple change could boost incentives on both the supply and the demand side of the equation: allow plans to bid to provide coverage for core hospital, physician, and prescription drug services, as they do now, at any price they choose. Eliminate the controls that do not allow them to pass full savings along to enrollees. But at the same time determine and deliver to enrollees a single-purpose, refundable subsidy—financed through the same combination of worker and employer payroll taxes, general revenues, and seniors' premiums as is enrollment in Medicare under the current system—which would be pegged to the bid premium of the second least expensive plan in the region. The subsidy at the second-least expensive plan's cost means that there will be more plan capacity at this zero-price point, and also ensures that there will be a choice between two plans for enrollees who want the zero-out-of-pocket-cost option.[129] Enrollees can still choose to pick a more expensive plan and pay the difference if they wish. And all plans should be paid "risk-adjusted" premiums—plans that take on sicker patients should be paid more, and plans with healthier patients should be paid less. This would incentivize plans to keep their premium prices down.

Putting Consumer Choice into Health Care

Health care is an enormous subject about which CED and others have written extensively. We do, however, believe that a few basic changes would modernize our system and also assure a safety net of access to care. Beyond reforming Medicare, allowing cost-conscious working-age consumers to choose their health care coverage could drive plans and providers to seek greater efficiency and lower costs. Consumers should have real choices among a variety of competing insurance plans. One size does not fit all; consumers have different preferences and expectations for care depending on their needs and where they live.

The government's intervention in health care should focus on setting standards of coverage and care quality, enforcing sound consumer protections, and ensuring the competitive playing field is fair, to prevent a "race to the bottom" dynamic. Minimal rules and risk adjustment can also ensure plans accept consumers at uniform premiums, regardless of pre-existing conditions. Plans that cover more costly risks should be rewarded for doing so through higher premium revenue. In contrast, we believe that provision of care and administration of the delivery of care are most effectively done through the private sector.

Government shouldn't try to protect the status quo. The diversity of plans that will appear, aimed at meeting consumer needs, will disrupt traditional plan and provider models. This is essential to increase quality and slow the growth of costs. In particular, the perverse fee-for-service model dominant in health care today will come under fire in a competitive market. Fee-for-service health care shackles competition and process improvement, and encourages overuse and waste—inefficiencies usually avoided in more open markets.

Allowing consumers more access points through which to choose and purchase insurance will help drive information in the market. Private exchanges or individual insurance brokers could offer services to consumers who prefer such relationships. Let market competition—bounded by appropriate safeguards against price discrimination—determine which kinds of information and guidance consumers want. We need true choice for people residing in more sparsely populated rural areas.

Information, not regulation, should guide the physician–patient relationship. Big data and greater access to information could improve the decisions made by both physicians and patients. Unleashing consumer choice in health care would improve access to, and the quality and cost of, health care for working–age citizens and their dependents, and over the long term ensure a sustainable health care system.

The aim should be to foster consumer choice, which will drive higher quality service at lower cost. Today, Medicare underwrites a perverse "fee-for-service" model for health care that has little incentive to reduce costs. Shifting consumers to a system that allows them to choose the plans that best meet their needs could potentially be transformative in health care, bending the cost curve and reducing the current unsustainable growth of costs under traditional Medicare.

The traditional fee-for-service Medicare plan should become one option among the many. Medicare administrators (the Centers for Medicare and Medicaid Services, or CMS) should be responsible for computing the price of a Medicare premium on a comparable basis, including all the elements of cost that would be borne by private Medicare Advantage plans—which they essentially do today in computing the "benchmark." They also should be responsible for using risk adjustment to compensate for the possibility that traditional Medicare would have an enrolled population that is more or less costly to cover than those of private Medicare Advantage plans. If traditional Medicare is more expensive than the second-lowest bid, then beneficiaries should pay the excess to continue with traditional coverage, as they would any more expensive choice, and have the option to save money by enrolling in a private plan. (Special provision should be made, of course, for current low-income beneficiaries, so that they can continue affordably with their current traditional FFS Medicare providers if they so choose.)

As competition drives plans to provide the health care that seniors want at lower cost, the cost that the federal government must pay for coverage under all Medicare plans, including traditional fee-for-service Medicare, will drop—as will the amount that workers must pay in payroll taxes and in general revenues to finance that coverage. Thus, the savings will be shared throughout the entire economy—the federal government, workers, and seniors. (See the summary of our proposal in table 6.1.[130]) The federal government's share of the savings will contribute to reducing the upward march of the nation's public debt burden, and therefore to the essential goal of making American capitalism sustainable.

Reduce Spending and Raise Revenues

Without serious reform of health care entitlements—particularly to reduce the skyrocketing cost of the Medicare program—America will remain in failing fiscal health. As the fastest growing component of the federal budget (and a large portion of it), Medicare is the driver of our long-term budget problem. Reforming Medicare is a *necessary* condition of regaining fiscal health.

But health care isn't the only reform that's needed. The debt burden already is too large and it is beginning to grow still larger; and restructuring our massive and complex health care system will take a long time. The growth of the debt burden already has an almost irresistible head of steam. To head off the growth of the gap between how much the federal government spends and how much it collects quickly enough, the nation needs to reduce other outlays and increase revenues. The key areas on which business leaders should focus their efforts are described in the following section.[131]

Domestic discretionary spending. The Budget Control Act of 2011 (BCA) imposed ten years of caps on domestic discretionary spending—that is, spending determined annually, largely funding for the various federal departments and agencies. Those cuts essentially met the targets set by the DRTF and other experts. However, the additional automatic cuts through sequestration (triggered by the failure of the so-called "Supercommittee" of the Congress, created by the BCA, to agree on $1.2 trillion of deficit reduction), which were scheduled to go into effect in January 2013, would slash discretionary spending far below those levels. Congress has backtracked on those excessive cuts in two subsequent partial budget agreements, covering four fiscal years. CED believes those cuts can be avoided in a sensible, comprehensive plan for addressing America's remaining fiscal challenges.

Instead, Congress could undertake a regular, systematic analysis of each area of discretionary spending to identify those programs that deserve reauthorization and those that require changes to be made more efficient. Such periodic reviews will improve the effectiveness and accountability of government. This is the "congressional oversight" that once was a basic element of the annual appropriations process—and should be again.

When applied thoughtfully, public-private partnerships can be an important source of additional funding for productivity-enhancing public investments in this era of tight budgets.[132]

Defense spending. Experts from across the political spectrum believe that the procurement, health, and retirement components of the U.S. defense budget require major reforms. But analogous to what has happened to domestic discretionary spending, defense spending has been beset by the "sequester." These programs should be targeted for reform in periodic congressional reviews such as the ones described above. However, streamlining waste here won't yield major savings in excess of those already mandated by the spending caps—much less the additional "sequester." In particular, the large procurement budget is a part of the annual appropriations process, which already has been cut along with domestic discretionary spending in the caps. And defense spending already has been cut to less than 3.5% of GDP, around a post-World War II low, while national security is an important concern. In short, defense discretionary spending should be rigorously scrutinized in the same careful process as domestic spending, to attain all possible efficiencies and savings that are consistent with our national security.

Other mandatory spending. Many federal programs run on autopilot, with little or no recurring oversight by Congress. Several reforms could constrain the growth of these programs and improve their effectiveness:

- Implement a package of farm program reforms;
- Adjust the retirement age for career military members so it is consistent with federal civilian retirement;
- Reform civilian retirement by calculating benefits based on a retiree's annual salary from his or her highest five years of government service, and increase employee contributions to the defined retirement benefit to be more consistent with the private sector;
- Raise fees to pay for aviation security;
- Adopt a more accurate inflation measurement to calculate cost-of-living-adjustments (COLAs) for all federal programs;
- Cease production of dollar bills and the one-cent piece, while increasing production of dollar coins;
- Index mandatory user fees to inflation;
- Restructure the power marketing administrations to charge market rates;
- Sell non-hydropower Tennessee Valley Authority electric utility assets to private investors;
- Reform the Postal Service; and
- Sell unneeded federal property.

Social Security. Like Medicare modernization, Social Security reform should not be approached from the vantage point of deficit reduction but rather with the goal of securing and strengthening a critical foundation for retirement for future generations. Without adjustments, the program will soon reach a point at which benefits must be slashed across the board or large transfers from general funds will be required—changing the fundamental nature of the program from the earned benefit that Americans have always insisted upon. For many reasons and from every standpoint, it would be irresponsible to run the program's trust fund into the ground by postponing reform until the very last minute. Accordingly, both parties in the Congress should work together with the President to adjust benefits and enhance revenues to set the program back on sound financial footing.

Recommended changes to the program to strengthen it for future generations include:

- Gradually raise the maximum earned income subject to the payroll tax to cover 90 percent of all wages, and maintain that share in later years;
- Use a more accurate calculation of annual COLAs (which should apply to all indexed programs, including the tax code);
- Implement modest additional means testing for high-income beneficiaries;
- Increase the minimum benefit to protect low-wage workers and those with interrupted careers;
- Index the benefit formula for increases in life expectancy; and
- Cover newly hired state and local workers under Social Security.

Tax reform, producing revenue increases. Every plausible route to long-term national fiscal sustainability includes realizing substantial additional revenue. But most tax reform experts inside and outside government believe policymakers can reform the tax code, and spur solid long-term economic growth, by streamlining the existing system, making it simpler, and turning it away from picking winners and losers as it does today. Business leaders should press the congressional tax-writing committees to build broad, bipartisan support around such a reform objective.

The Debt Reduction Task Force tax reform plan would radically simplify the current tax code and raise additional revenue. Outlined below are the core elements of the plan.

- There would be a two-bracket individual income tax with rates of 15 percent and 28 percent. Because there is no standard deduction or personal exemption, the 15 percent rate applies to the first dollar of income.[133]

- The corporate tax rate will be a flat 28 percent, instead of the current 35 percent top rate.

- Capital gains and dividends will be taxed as ordinary income (with a top rate of 28 percent), excluding the first $1,000 of realized net capital gains (or losses).[134]

- To replace the overly complex Earned Income Tax Credit (EITC) and the personal exemptions, the standard deduction, and the child credit:
  - Establish a flat refundable per child tax credit of $1,600 (higher than current law);
  - Retain the child and dependent care credit; and
  - Establish a refundable earnings credit similar in structure to the recent Making Work Pay credit, but substantially larger.[135]

- Replace the current system of itemized deductions, which disproportionately subsidizes the housing and charitable giving of upper-income taxpayers, with the following changes:
  - Provide a flat 15-percent refundable tax credit for charitable contributions and for up to $25,000 per year (not indexed) mortgage interest on a primary residence.
  - Eliminate the deduction for state and local taxes.
  - Provide a flat, 15-percent refundable tax credit or a deduction (for those in the higher bracket) for contributions to retirement savings accounts up to 20 percent of earnings or a maximum of $20,000.

- Include as taxable income 100 percent of Social Security benefits, but at the same time create a non-refundable credit for Social Security beneficiaries equal to 15 percent of the current standard deduction; and create a non-refundable credit equal to 15 percent of an individual's Social Security benefits.

- Phase out, over ten years, the tax exclusion for employer-sponsored health insurance benefits. (This provision would be superseded by enactment of CED's health reform proposal for working-age families—see sidebar in this chapter, "Putting Consumer Choice into Health Care.")
- Limit miscellaneous itemized deductions to the amount exceeding 5 percent of AGI (increased from 2 percent in current law).
- Eliminate the alternative minimum tax (AMT).
- Increase the gas tax by 15 cents and index it to inflation, dedicating the revenue to the highway trust fund.
- Increase taxes on tobacco and alcohol.

Enactment of these reforms would greatly simplify the tax code by aligning the top individual, capital gains, and dividend tax rates with a significantly reduced corporate tax rate and elimination of the AMT. Most individuals wouldn't have to file an annual tax return anymore,[136] beyond an initial declaration of status. That's because the most commonly taken deductions are either converted into refundable credits, determined solely based on the number of children and earnings, or can be deducted only above a substantial floor. Despite a low top rate of 28 percent, this tax plan will increase progressivity and will raise the requisite revenue to reduce the debt.

■ ■ ■

This plan for reducing spending and rationalizing revenues addresses the nation's fiscal problem with a balanced and workable approach. The plan also shows that the challenge can be met if lawmakers demonstrate leadership, put everything on the table, and accept the need for both sides to compromise. Making the needed changes will not be easy, but they would improve the quality and efficiency of government and strengthen the economy for all Americans. The nation must face up to its looming debt crisis. America's debt problem has advanced to the stage where it can pose an existential threat. The nation needs substantial fiscal reforms soon.

In the fight for fiscal reform in Washington, business leaders must step in as catalysts for change. Business leaders have credibility on these issues, because they can demonstrate how they have recognized financial problems and made difficult decisions on their day jobs. They should use their credibility—their bully pulpit—to pressure for needed reforms. And business leaders should build that credibility by acknowledging the self-evident: that the budget problem has grown so large that *all* Americans—their companies clearly included—must step up and play their appropriate roles in putting the nation on a sound fiscal course.

American capitalism has made our nation the financial bedrock of the world, the moral leader in international behavior and relationships, and the largest economy on earth. All of that is at risk if the budget problem is allowed to grow while our elected policymakers remain oblivious and complacent. U.S. capitalism cannot survive in a nation awash with debt. Success in addressing this fiscal problem would be monumental in its own right—and would be vivid, undisputable proof that our political system—and capitalism—are sustainable and can work for every American.

7

Regulation to Build Trust in Capitalism

IN THE IDEAL WORLD there would be no need for regulations. Markets and the overall economy would operate efficiently and fairly. But experience has taught us that there are times when for a variety of reasons regulations are required, and their use should be restricted to those instances. The challenge then is to ensure that regulations contribute to, rather than undermine, the economic and social good—that their benefits exceed their costs. This chapter looks at the proper role for regulation and for business leaders in improving regulatory outcomes.

Regulations serve as the documented "rules of the game" in a democratic society and a market-based, capitalist economy. Regulations provide a legal framework to establish and enforce property rights and standards of behavior. In addition to fiscal policy, they are another tool the government can use to steer markets toward economic outcomes that are in the public interest, where free markets on their own may fail to do the job. The major justifications for and roles of regulations are: (1) to address "market failures" where true costs and benefits to society (the entire range of "stakeholders") are not reflected correctly in market prices; (2) to prevent monopolization of industry and "level the playing field" to support greater competition and innovation; and (3) to ensure consumer, worker, and investor health and safety, transparency in information about goods and services, and a fair distribution of net benefits. These are all public-interest goals not naturally served by purely self-interested, private-sector motives. Hence, regulation can be an obvious, well-justified role for government that Adam Smith understood and underscored centuries ago. At its theoretical ideal, government regulation can facilitate the workings of the economy, to promote a healthy level of competition and "vibrancy" in the economy, and to ensure resources flow easily and toward the uses most valued by society.

To approach this ideal, the regulatory process should follow these core principles:

1. A regulation should be created only to address an urgent and material market failure.[137]

2. New regulations must be clear, unique and non-overlapping or conflicting with other existing regulations.

3. The design process of regulations must be open and transparent, and include subject-matter experts as well as academics and impacted parties.

4. There must be robust *a priori* testing of any practical implementation constraints and areas of unintended consequence, as part of a rigorous cost-benefit analysis and period of review and public comment. Measured costs should include the cumulative compliance burden on affected stakeholders.

5. There must be a full commitment of resources and support commensurate with the importance of the regulation, to facilitate proper ex-post oversight and evaluation.

6. In addition, the regulators themselves need proper resources and support. The legislators who mandate regulation need expert support so that the laws they write do not require unworkable or excessively expensive regulations.

In the real world, it's not easy living up to the theoretical ideal of well-founded regulations that guide markets to unambiguously improved outcomes for society. Writing regulations is an activity inherently fraught with tensions and beset by competing interests. These regulations often are designed to favor the most politically powerful incumbent businesses—another manifestation of "crony capitalism"—to the detriment of new business formation and the innovation and productivity growth of the overall economy. Special interests often are successful in cloaking themselves in public-interest costumes—a phenomenon economist Bruce Yandle has dubbed the "Bootleggers and Baptists" practice of regulatory policy.[138] In this way policymakers and the general public easily can be fooled into writing regulations that cater to special interests above society's best interests.

In actual practice, regulations often "throw sand in the gears," rather than "grease the wheels," of productive business activity. Regulations can be difficult to understand and comply with, particularly for new and small businesses. Regulations motivated by popular concern and misunderstanding, but developed without subject-area expert input and experience, can slow innovation and economic growth. A mass of regulations intended to address small economic problems cumulatively can create complexity and confusion. A Gallup poll (Figure 7.1) shows that the share of Americans who feel there is "too much" government regulation of business and industry has grown over the past decade to around half, compared with only about a quarter who say there's "too little."[139] This result probably has much more to do with Americans' perception about the complexity of regulations with which they have to deal in their real lives, rather than their questioning the stated purposes of those regulations and the appropriate role of government.

So what can be done to have regulations better serve the needs and wants of our economy and society? How can regulatory policy better support and sustain our system of capitalism? How can business leaders improve regulatory policy and operations?

There are a few pragmatic steps that business leaders should advocate and policymakers should adopt to improve regulatory policy. First, in the development of any new regulation there needs to be more focus on

FIGURE 7.1   U.S. Public Opinion on the Level of Government Regulation of Business and Industry

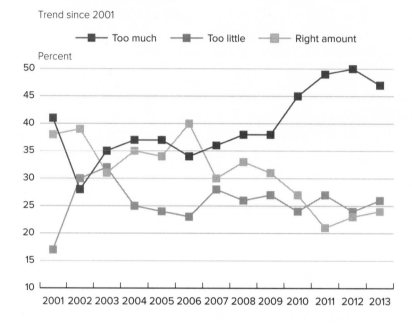

Source: Gallup, "In U.S., Half Still Say Gov't Regulates Business Too Much," September 18, 2015, http://www.gallup.com/poll/185609/half-say-gov-regulates-business.aspx.

the public interest justification and the goals or principles to be served. Second, ideally those goals and principles should be defined so that they are measurable and so that regulations can be designed, maintained, monitored—and periodically updated, as necessary. This will ensure that regulations continually serve their purposes. And, finally, the entire government regulatory process—as regulations are being debated, developed, renewed, or reconsidered—needs to be made more open and transparent to all stakeholders affected, and to make full use of expert input. By making the regulatory process more inclusive, regulations (and government in general) will be viewed as, and will in fact *be*, more impartial and supportive of the public interest.

Regulations are needed where private markets left on their own would lead to socially suboptimal allocations of resources—either because social values (costs or benefits) are not fully captured in market prices, or because the distributional outcomes of unfettered markets are undesirable. Determining the broad justification for a regulation is a good starting point for policymakers, followed by articulating the more specific purpose or goal, followed by the determination and consideration of alternative policy approaches—be they different types of regulations or fiscal (tax and spending) policies—or doing nothing (if policy responses would do more harm than good). Such a regulatory process would be more transparent, more consistent, and less prone to hijacking and manipulation by special interests.

An Appropriate Balance Between (Broad) Principles and (Narrow) Rules

Our current system of regulation is heavily *rules based*, which means that regulations are highly specific and narrowly focused. Rules-based regulation can have the advantage that it provides clarity and specificity to businesses and regulators, such that both know where they stand in any conceivable circumstance. However, rules-based regulation can have disadvantages as well. Overly specific rules can stifle innovation that could lead to new, more-efficient ways to comply with the actual purpose of the regulation. As an extreme example, regulations that specify precisely the technology, often termed "best available technology" or BAT, to be used to reduce pollution can have limited payoff and might even discourage the development of more-efficient and cheaper technology.[140] Or a highly specific rule might create an opportunity to comply with the letter of the regulation while violating its spirit.[141] Such overly specific regulation might lead to a cat-and-mouse iterative contest between the regulator and the regulated, wasting valuable economic resources on both sides as still more new rules follow on sequential attempts to circumvent those rules.

Boundaries that might be deemed desirable at the birth of a regulation may later serve as a straight-jacket, preventing an industry from

SIDEBAR 7.1

How to Analyze a Regulation (Before It's Born)

In their book, *Regulation: A Primer*, Susan Dudley (who headed the OIRA during the George W. Bush Administration) and Jerry Brito suggest logical steps to analyze a proposed regulation, beginning with the existential question: What is the regulation intended to accomplish? Does it adjust or correct a market failure preventing the private market from delivering an optimal outcome for the economy and society? If so, what is the nature of the failure, and is a regulatory approach (and what type) the best way to correct or adjust for the failure, considering both the benefits and costs? What kinds of evidence can be gathered and considered to evaluate the likelihood of success before a regulation is established?

1. Identify a significant market failure or systemic problem;
2. Identify alternative approaches;
3. Choose the regulatory action that maximizes net benefits;
4. Base the proposal on strong scientific or technical grounds;
5. Understand the effects of the regulation on different populations; and
6. Respect individual choice and property rights.

evolving and innovating in response to changing economic conditions and price signals. At its worst, such overspecificity could suppress innovation not just in the technology to comply with the regulation, but also in the underlying industry itself. It could be a tool of crony capitalism to stifle competition, protecting old industry from innovators who ultimately could take their new ideas to our nation's international competitors.

A broadly different approach followed in some other countries is *principles-based* regulation. Legislation would mandate, and regulators would produce, rules that provide greater flexibility. For example, a rule might specify a maximum amount of pollution that could be emitted, but firms

FIGURE 7.2   Recommended Process of Regulatory Analysis

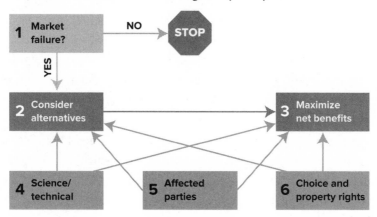

Source: Susan Dudley and Jerry Brito, *Regulation: A Primer.* Arlington, VA: Mercatus Center at George Mason University. Available online at: http://mercatus.org/sites/default/files/RegulatoryPrimer_ DudleyBrito_0.pdf.

In other words, justify a role for government, find the approach (regulatory or otherwise) most likely to improve the economic outcome and maximize *net* benefit to society, and then consider (and address if needed) any undesirable distributional effects.

could find the best way to meet that standard. This would open the door to competition, innovation, and higher incomes and living standards, all the while simplifying regulation and cutting the cost of compliance.

Neither rules- nor principles-based regulation is a complete and unalterable answer. A healthy balance must be struck. While principles-based regulation can allow flexibility for efficiency and innovation, it must also be substantive enough that the objective of the regulation is certain and enforceable. In some instances—such as the formula for the calculation of the annual percentage rate (APR) in lending regulation—explicit rules inevitably will be necessary.[142] But when possible, a more balanced approach of writing clear rules that promote economic principles, without inefficiently constraining private-sector decisions on how to comply with the rules, would be a promising and fundamental switch from the current way of regulating.

Another dimension of basing regulations on principles is the use of market forces. Economists of all political persuasions favor regulation through more flexible, market-driven approaches. For example, in the case of environmental policy, setting pollution charges (taxes) instead of imposing rules requiring specific types of pollution-reducing equipment. Using the price system allows markets to efficiently "self-correct" in response to newly recognized social costs and benefits, while preserving the fluctuating market signals contained in the private component of prices. Market-based approaches also facilitate the collection of "real-time" information on the behavioral effects of these programs—all the better to inform the retrospective review of regulations.

Better Data for Creation of Regulations, and for Post-Reviews

For a regulation to contribute to, rather than undermine, the economic and social good, the benefits of the regulation must exceed its costs. To the greatest possible degree the comparison of costs and benefits should be explicit. To improve regulatory policy and ensure that regulations achieve their goals, policy analysts and regulators need better information— higher-quality data for economic analysis to plan and evaluate regulations. Furthermore, all regulations must be reviewed periodically to ensure that they continue to meet their objectives. Such retrospective review has been mandated by executive order, but follow-through has been weak.

Making cost-benefit comparisons is challenging, but current practice can be improved. For instance, during the last few years, researchers have been making strides in understanding and measuring the economic effects of regulation, but government regulatory analysts and the methodologies they use haven't always kept pace. On the cost side of the ledger, analysts aren't even able to determine whether regulations will create jobs or destroy them, says Keith Hall, current director of the Congressional Budget Office.[143] But assessing the benefits of regulations can be even more challenging. As many observers have pointed out, analysts can be more confident in their assessments of the costs in reduced economic output of new environmental policies (for example) than of benefits, in part because benefits are remote and uncertain and reach into areas with moral overtones.[144] Even when the benefits are more economic than social, and therefore more readily expressed in dollar terms, decision makers might legitimately disagree over assessing how many future dollars of benefit are required to justify one dollar of current cost.

More "micro-level" data—that is, data about individual affected businesses or households—can help.[145] Researchers recently used such data, for instance, to study the effects of environmental regulations in isolation from other factors that affect pollution emissions, such as trade, productivity, and consumer preferences. The researchers used factory-level records from the Census Bureau and the Environmental Protection Agency (EPA). Their study, a "model-driven decomposition" of the causes of the observed pollution changes, found that environmental regulation explains 75 percent or more of the observed reduction in pollution emissions from U.S. manufacturing from 1990 to 2008.[146]

Evaluating the anticipated impacts of a proposed new regulation should be just the first step. Regulations must be evaluated retrospectively, as well. A regulation can become obsolete and even counterproductive. In contrast to all government discretionary spending programs, and many mandatory programs, existing regulations do not come up for annual reconsideration and reauthorization. The regulatory system should adopt a continuous, systematic review of the existing regulatory portfolio. While an executive order has directed agencies to conduct more ex-post evaluation,[147] such "retrospective review" is not yet practiced routinely and systematically—and has not been enforced through legislation. (A few legislative proposals have been introduced but not enacted.[148])

Emblematic of the challenges of both initial and retrospective review is the "self-review" process of regulatory agencies. This process is both costly and time consuming, and provides little incentive to be self-critical. An April 2014 Government Accountability Office (GAO) report found that the regulatory agencies had made some progress in

FIGURE 7.3   Prevalence of Types of Reported Retrospective Analysis Outcomes for Executive Agencies that Implemented Final Actions from January 2011–August 2013

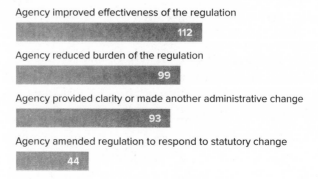

Source: From U.S. Government Accountability Office, GAO-14-268, *Reexamining Regulations: Agencies Often Made Regulatory Changes, but Could Strengthen Linkages to Performance, Goals,* April 2014, Figure 2, page 13 (http://www.gao.gov/assets/670/662517.pdf).

retrospective reviews and that the reviews often improved the clarity and effectiveness of regulations and reduced the compliance costs, but that more guidance was needed to improve the transparency and usefulness of the information to policymakers and the general public and to tie the findings to the agencies' performance and priority goals.[149] (See Figure 7.3, "Prevalence of Types of Reported Retrospective Analysis Outcomes . . .") One way to circumvent the tendencies of agencies to be defensive about their own regulations in any review process would be to expand the scope of the White House Office of Information and Regulatory Affairs (OIRA).[150] The OIRA could select existing regulations for the earliest review, guided by priorities set by the Congress. Those priorities could include the "significance" of the regulations as measured by the cost impact in dollar terms, and the length of time that the regulations have been in force, and the degree of public demand solicited through the current comment process.

Improving ex-post review of regulation will require investment. Providing more resources to regulatory agencies should not have to lead to more regulation—it can, and should, underwrite better and smarter regulation. Better data are needed to facilitate stronger and more-frequent review of regulations, and therefore the cleaning-out or improvement of obsolete or deficient ones.

A More Inclusive Regulatory Process

The regulatory process can be more impartial, transparent to stakeholders and the public, and comprehensive (that is, broadly applicable, without exemptions), and can avoid capture by regulators or special interests. It needs political and funding support even when it must undertake controversial tasks. Seven principles for regulatory governance, developed by the Organization for Economic Cooperation and Development (OECD) in 2014, should guide the regulatory process.[151] They are:

1. *Role clarity:* An effective regulator must have clear objectives, with clear and linked functions and the mechanisms to coordinate with other relevant bodies to achieve the desired regulatory outcomes.

2. *Preventing undue influence and maintaining trust:* Integrity should imbue the regulatory process, to ensure that there is confidence in the regulatory regime.

3. *Decision-making and governing body structure for independent regulators:* Regulators require governance arrangements that ensure their effective functioning preserve its regulatory integrity and deliver the regulatory objectives of its mandate.

4. *Accountability and transparency:* Businesses and citizens expect the delivery of regulatory outcomes from government and regulatory agencies, and the proper use of public authority and resources to achieve them. Regulators are generally accountable to three groups of stakeholders: (i) ministers and the legislature; (ii) regulated entities; and (iii) the public.

5. *Engagement:* Good regulators have established mechanisms for engagement with stakeholders as part of achieving their objectives. The knowledge of regulated sectors and the businesses and citizens affected by regulatory schemes assists to regulate effectively.

OECD Guiding Principles for Regulatory Quality and Performance

In 2012, the OECD Regulatory Policy Committee issued 12 recommendations for regulatory policy reform. They are:

1. Commit at the highest political level to an explicit whole-of-government policy for regulatory quality. The policy should have clear objectives and frameworks for implementation to ensure that, if regulation is used, the economic, social and environmental benefits justify the costs, distributional effects are considered and the net benefits are maximized.

2. Adhere to principles of open government, including transparency and participation in the regulatory process to ensure that regulation serves the public interest and is informed by the legitimate needs of those interested in and affected by regulation. This includes providing meaningful opportunities (including online) for the public to contribute to the process of preparing draft regulatory proposals and to the quality of the supporting analysis. Governments should ensure that regulations are comprehensible and clear and that parties can easily understand their rights and obligations.

3. Establish mechanisms and institutions to actively provide oversight of regulatory policy procedures and goals, support and implement regulatory policy, and thereby foster regulatory quality.

4. Integrate Regulatory Impact Assessment (RIA) into the early stages of the policy process for the formulation of new regulatory proposals. Clearly identify policy goals, and evaluate if regulation is necessary and how it can be most effective and efficient in achieving those goals. Consider means other than regulation and identify the tradeoffs of the different approaches analyzed to identify the best approach.

5. Conduct systematic program reviews of the stock of significant regulation against clearly defined policy goals, including

consideration of costs and benefits, to ensure that regulations remain up to date, cost-justified, cost-effective, and consistent and [deliver] the intended policy objectives.

6. Regularly publish reports on the performance of regulatory policy and reform programs and the public authorities applying the regulations. Such reports should also include information on how regulatory tools such as Regulatory Impact Assessment (RIA), public consultation practices and reviews of existing regulations are functioning in practice.

7. Develop a consistent policy covering the role and functions of regulatory agencies in order to provide greater confidence that regulatory decisions are made on an objective, impartial and consistent basis, without conflict of interest, bias or improper influence.

8. Ensure the effectiveness of systems for the review of the legality and procedural fairness of regulations, and of decisions made by bodies empowered to issue regulatory sanctions. Ensure that citizens and businesses have access to these systems of review at reasonable cost and receive decisions in a timely manner.

9. As appropriate apply risk assessment, risk management, and risk communication strategies to the design and implementation of regulations to ensure that regulation is targeted and effective. Regulators should assess how regulations will be given effect and should design responsive implementation and enforcement strategies.

10. Where appropriate promote regulatory coherence through coordination mechanisms between the supra national, the national, and subnational levels of government. Identify cross cutting regulatory issues at all levels of government, to promote coherence between regulatory approaches and avoid duplication or conflict of regulations.

11. Foster the development of regulatory management capacity and performance at subnational levels of government.

12. In developing regulatory measures, give consideration to all relevant international standards and frameworks for cooperation in the same field and, where appropriate, their likely effects on parties outside the jurisdiction.

6. *Funding:* The amount and source of funding for a regulator will determine its organization and operations. It should not influence the regulatory decisions and the regulator should be enabled to be impartial and efficient to achieve its objectives.

7. *Performance evaluation:* It is important that regulators are aware of the impacts of their regulatory actions and decisions. This helps drive improvements and enhance systems and processes internally. It also demonstrates the effectiveness of the regulator to whom it is accountable and helps to build confidence in the regulatory system.

Improving stakeholder engagement in the regulatory process also will improve its governance. Currently, stakeholder participation in rulemaking is mostly a one-way street. Advances in online technology have certainly allowed more of the general public to become aware of regulations (both proposed and in place) and submit comments about them. Though descriptions of regulatory policies in the pipeline are provided to the public and comments are solicited, there is little evidence that feedback collected via public comment is systematically accounted for in actual decision-making.

Business leaders who care about the broader national interest as well as their narrower industry point of view (and who can reconcile the two) should be pro-active and get more involved in the regulatory process, participating from start to finish in the development of new regulations, and on a continuous basis in the administration and evaluation of existing regulations. Regulatory policy would be improved by such informed input and feedback coming from those who both have to deal with the regulations and are the engine of our economy. The more the public and private sectors can communicate and collaborate, the better regulation will work for our economy.

THE ROLE OF GOVERNMENT REGULATION
IN THE FINANCIAL SECTOR

We discuss financial regulation specifically here for two reasons: a) the financial sector is critical to the day-to-day functioning of any developed economy, from protecting assets to supporting credit intermediation, and such vital functions require regulatory oversight; and b) the financial sector is seen around the world as having played a central role in the 2008 economic and financial crisis, which is an important cause of *popular* hostility to the entire free-market capitalist system.

There were many links in the causal chain that led to the 2008 global economic crisis—so many, in fact, that it is exceedingly difficult to distinguish the ultimate causes from the mere effects, and to assess the relative roles of the various causes. The U.S. financial system certainly played a material and highly visible role, but it was not alone. Importantly, however, many of the mistakes made by U.S. finance were surprisingly basic. The perceived centrality of exotic financial instruments overstates the reality. The result has been a regulatory response that could well be found in future years to have increased complexity and compliance burden on peripheral issues and symptoms, while leaving untouched or even worsening some of the prime movers of this crisis—and possibly the next one.

Healthy finance is fundamental to all of the objectives of our system of capitalism. New and innovative businesses need access to capital. Families with modest incomes who are willing to make a viable commitment need help to establish equity in their homes, and to deal with the vagaries that they encounter in their daily lives. As part of the American value system we support home ownership more strongly than other countries do.

It would be imprudent in the extreme to subject the U.S. economy to another wrenching crisis similar to 2008. Both policymakers and lenders need to be responsible. Taking some risk is in the American character, but policymakers and lenders need to ensure that individuals are not encouraged to take risks that they cannot prudentially manage. Yet in the buildup of the financial crisis, some financial institutions made the most fundamental errors: lending money to people who had no income and were asked for no documentation; lending long and borrowing very short; failing to do fundamental due diligence; borrowing in one currency and lending in another; lending at fixed interest rates and borrowing at floating rates; committing to be a "lender of last resort," and thereby accepting enormous potential liabilities, for literally just a few basis points of fees.

With those fundamental business miscalculations at the root of the crisis, focusing on exotic financial instruments as the ultimate cause can lead to neglecting or weakening what should be some of the most important remedies. For example, a lack of liquidity was cited by many experts as the proximate cause of the financial contagion in 2008, but an unintended consequence of purported remedies since has been to reduce liquidity in many important market instruments and products. Thus, in a crisis, financial and nonfinancial institutions may not be able to fund themselves. This increased liquidity risk has caused institutions to keep significantly more cash and cash equivalents on hand than good management would normally dictate. This reduces resources available to the economy and reduces hiring and employment. Further, as of 2016, only one single institution remains to settle the single most important market liquidity instrument—U.S. Treasury securities. Thus, rather than reducing systemic risks by strengthening the key areas of vulnerability in the U.S. financial system, the complex web of new regulation drains resources without addressing some fundamental problems behind the crisis, while causing and creating some serious new systemic risks to the taxpayer, and holding back the recovery of the U.S. economy.

Policy to contain the 2008 crisis included a number of unprecedented infusions of cash and financial guarantees, but these were easily mischaracterized to suggest that "Wall Street" (from small commercial banks to large investment houses and perhaps even insurance companies and other regulated financial institutions) received protection at the expense of "Main Street," i.e., the taxpayer. The popular narrative continues that the taxpayers lost vast sums of money due to the support of banks in general. Some financial institutions absolutely needed the liquidity that was supplied on an emergency basis. But there is little awareness that the number of such institutions was small, and that many large banks were required to accept taxpayer money so as not to stigmatize the troubled institutions and thereby to subject them to panic and depositor runs. Ultimately, the U.S. Treasury earned significant positive returns on the money loaned, but this has not been widely reported.[152] The average citizen remains uncomfortable, uncertain, and anxious. The perception of the U.S. financial system as the source of all of the nation's economic problems has damaged the faith of many citizens in financial institutions, government, and even some fundamentals of capitalism. The crisis and its aftermath thus pose a very direct threat to the sustainability of capitalism. Of course, had the crisis not been contained, the economy and capitalism would have been put to an even greater test. That is just one of many reasons why financial crises are dangerous, and to be avoided even at some cost.

A financial crisis on the scale of the U.S. economy would not only wreak havoc in our country, but also immediately transmit and impose massive spillover costs to the rest of the global economy and society. So balance is needed, and part of that balance is that government must keep the nation's overall loan portfolio sound, through regulation if necessary.

Given the potential risk, many voices suggest that the financial sector needs more regulation—more boundaries placed upon it—because large institutions in trouble can put the economy at risk. Following this approach, regulated financial institutions would be small utilities whose failures could not disrupt daily lives, and the nature of their activities would be such as to meet only basic domestic financial needs. This would suggest that all financial innovation would take place outside of the regulated environment and that global financial services would be provided by non-U.S. financial institutions. However, there would be serious unintended consequences of this well-intentioned desire to make America safe again, and they would damage America's ability to compete, but even worse would create and heighten new existential systemic risks.

If all innovation takes place outside of the regulated environment then there would be virtually no transparency, no information, no controls, and no oversight. In particular, innovation taking place outside of the regulated sphere would mean that new products and activity would occur outside of the oversight, knowledge, and control of the regulators.

In addition, if the banks became small utilities they would not be able to service today's fundamental economic needs—like a post office restricted to manual technology. This would mean that to help them compete in global markets, many U.S. companies—big and small— would have to rely on support for their commercial activity from global players—who with the departure of the U.S. institutions would be Chinese, French, Japanese, Russian, and Spanish. Although the average taxpayer may be indifferent to forcing all trade finance into the hands of foreign financial institutions, many exporters and companies with international activities might prefer to have financial partners whose commitments align with U.S. priorities, rather than those of other governments.

Virtually every aspect of the Dodd-Frank legislation is highly controversial. We do not aspire to resolve all of that controversy. However, there is one issue with respect to the post-Dodd-Frank financial structure that calls for early, perhaps even urgent, consideration. It may be simple and straightforward, but it flies in the face of one of the most intense public impressions of the financial crisis.

Legislation should restore and even expand the Federal Reserve's lender-of-last-resort capabilities, for banks and non-bank financial institutions. Such a step would not be inconsistent with ending "too big to fail," because failing large non-bank financial firms could be reorganized or liquidated while preserving the stability of the financial system. The real issue has never been "too big to fail." It is, rather, "too big to fail in a haphazard fashion." There are tools in place, even some before Dodd-Frank, that would have allowed for orderly liquidation.

The importance of this step should not be understated. The financial crisis of 2008 was years in the making, but erupted suddenly when a series of events literally "spooked" the market and caused institutions that supplied short-term liquidity to withdraw it. Liquidity providers to institutions that had imprudently chosen to lend long and borrow short, and to act as lenders of last resort to other institutions, could not risk being the last in line should those challenged institutions' doors finally have closed. This triggered a frightening domino effect that quickly transferred to other activities, and in short order there was a serious contagion risk that saw basic financial service instruments starting to fail. Even top-ranked financial institutions began to have their letters of credit rejected or denied. A "China syndrome" global financial meltdown was literally in sight.

The American people have expressed extreme distaste for bailing out "bad actors." While the American taxpayer made a sizable profit on providing liquidity to the banking sector in the financial crisis, the mental soundbite for the populace was that bankers cost them massive amounts of money and then benefited undeservedly. However, the nature of contagion is that good actors suffer through the financial equivalent of guilt by association; dominoes begin to fall, knocking over the just with the unjust. With sound lender-of-last-resort authority in place, innocent-bystander institutions would not be at such severe risk. Creditors of financial institutions with sufficient collateral (valued under "normal market conditions") would not feel the compulsion to "run" on those institutions, which would have access to funds in crisis conditions because of the lender-of-last-resort authority.[153]

It is impossible to eliminate the risk of all future financial crises with any policy action, no matter how strong. No one can see the future, and so no one can ensure that any combination of loans, however apparently secure, will not go bad. Thus, the only totally foolproof approach would be to ban all leverage; and that radical step would sacrifice much investment and innovation that would suddenly be starved of financing. But the best possible balance of security and availability of credit for growth requires that future reforms address the fundamental elements of the financial system that really put taxpayers and capitalism at risk, not popular myths, and not some of the financial system's features that may appear to be more problematic than they really are.

As with all forms of regulatory policy, a balance must be struck between providing effective boundaries to keep private behavior more consistent with the public, broader good, but not so constraining on private decisions such that investment and innovation are stifled.

CONCLUSION

Three systemic reforms to the regulatory process would go a long way toward making regulations less costly (in economic, administrative, and psychic senses) and more effective:

- Striking a healthy balance between broader principles and narrow rules in conceptualizing and designing regulations;

- Improving data and analysis in both ex-ante and ex-post evaluations; and

- Making the entire regulatory process more inclusive to stakeholders.

Business leaders have long pressed policymakers to eliminate layers of regulations that constrain economic growth with little or no social upside. But this may appear to be the special interests of business complaining on their own behalf. Business leaders could better serve their own and the public interests by helping policymakers design and maintain regulations that promote greater competition and vibrancy in the market economy. They should focus the discussion, more strategically, on reforming the system of regulation itself. Building and maintaining better regulations requires investment in data and analysis, and good lines of communication and engagement with stakeholders—including business leaders and the broader public. This will drive long-term reforms that will benefit the economy and society.

A better regulatory system will stimulate innovation and economic growth—a key part of making capitalism sustainable. But perhaps even more importantly, it will reduce frustration by the regulated and will rebuild the public trust. Better regulation must be a high priority.

8

Sustainable Capitalism and the Global Economy

A KEY LESSON of this book is that making capitalism sustainable for the twenty-first century requires the will once again to pursue America's comparative advantages. If business and policy leaders can motivate all stakeholders to deepen their participation in our economic system, the United States would realize far more value—both economic and social. Actual *and potential* customers, employees, owners, suppliers, communities, and other stakeholders today are underutilized assets. Considering all of these constituencies in decision-making and formulating a long-term vision; making much-needed investments in developing employee skills that really matter in a global knowledge economy; reforming education to improve equality of opportunity; reducing cronyism and making government work once again; improving fiscal health so that government can build for the future and focus on the right priorities; and streamlining the entanglements of regulation that have grown like kudzu at the interface of business and society—this is essentially a game plan for investing in the human capital, social vibrancy, and the sheer enterprising spirit that has long underwritten American prosperity.

This game plan for making capitalism sustainable in the United States needs one more element, however. Capitalism today must be globally sustainable: As technology gradually but inexorably integrates national economies, U.S. capitalism must work in concert with other economic systems all around the world. The global flow of capital, trade, people, and ideas, coupled with advances in technology and communications, are twin genies of all modern economies, and they can't go back into the bottle. Trying to slow them would threaten prosperity. The boom in global trade over the last few decades has enhanced productivity (in part by fostering value chain specialization), expanded the size and reach of many markets, stimulated innovations in how companies operate and how managers manage, boosted the purchasing power and living standards of consumers, and raised wages broadly in exporting sectors.

Unfortunately, some families, particularly those living in smaller communities and working in import-vulnerable industries, have not shared fully in the benefits. This must be addressed. As discussed in Chapter 1, the globalization of trade and labor markets, and the digital technology revolution, have skewed the distribution of personal economic rewards—wealth and income—in society. The twin genies of modern capitalism have boosted the value of some skills but de-valued others, replaced or relocated millions of jobs, and changed the nature of work for millions more workers. These forces have suppressed wage gains for a wide swath of American working families while delivering outsized gains to a few. These shifts (along with the rapid growth in scale and scope of the financial sector) contribute to inequality, which has aroused the passions of the American public. In the decades ahead, advances in technology, even more than continued globalization, are likely to exacerbate all of these frictions.

Meeting the societal challenges sparked by technological change will require concerted action by businesses and governments, working together on real solutions. Society's leaders will need to develop mechanisms to identify and even anticipate shifts in the demand for workplace skills, as more and more work will use technological tools combined with human judgment. Decision makers will need to create institutions and policy tools that quickly can respond to mismatches in the supply of and demand for skills. In so doing, they must thoroughly overhaul an education system that is failing most U.S. children today.

Business and policy leaders also must advance a vision for financing and modernizing America's infrastructure. Finally, public and private thinking must put forward ideas for helping all Americans—urban and rural, young and old—to benefit from technological change. With the constantly accelerating pace of innovation and change, some segments of society fail to keep pace with technological advances, and so the next generation of leaders will need to focus on expanding digital inclusiveness.

But what are America's leaders to do about globalization? Globalization—the ever-widening mobility of capital, labor, goods, and even ideas—is the bane of many, and not just in America. Britain has voted to leave the European Union in large part to isolate itself from economic forces that many identify as the root cause of their lagging prosperity. Significant numbers of voters in France, the Netherlands, and other EU nations would like to do the same. Several nations in the Middle East are literally burning with rage against globalization. Anti-immigration sentiments have spiked in Europe and the United States. Polls suggest that as many as nine out of ten Americans want businesses to stop "offshoring" jobs. Globalization has generated so much prosperity, but also dislocation, fear, and anxiety. How do leaders meet the globalization dilemma?

The answer is balance. The anti-trade and anti-immigration rhetoric seen in the 2016 presidential campaign cycle is, in the view of CED, sadly misguided. Imposing trade restrictions and barriers, or unduly restricting immigration, is economically self-defeating. Rather than helping workers disadvantaged by globalization, policies that erect barriers to imports (or penalize companies for producing globally) in the end will disadvantage all Americans, and impair—not restore—U.S. prosperity. Doing so would surrender the higher standard of living Americans enjoy through lower-cost goods and higher-value, export-oriented jobs. The answer is not to retreat but to move forward, while working to balance the ledger of globalization. This will require business and policy leaders to better integrate trade and immigration in the real economy, and create and implement policies and programs that support workers and communities caught in the transitions inherent in globalization, and spread the gains of globalization more widely.

PUSH FOR GREATER EQUALIZATION OF TRADE AGREEMENTS

Ultimately, to achieve a successful, sustainable economy and prosperity, America needs to engage even more with the global economy. The value of world trade declined in 2015 (to $16.5 trillion, down from $19 trillion in 2014 according to the World Trade Organization) and the growth in the value of trade has been sluggish since the 2008 financial crisis, relative to trends just before.[154] But since the 1990s, global trade has grown, on average, twice as fast as global GDP. In 1990, exports of U.S. goods and services amounted to less than $600 billion, and imports to the United States a little more than $600 billion. In 2015, the United States exported nearly $2.4 trillion in goods and services (America has become a leading exporter of services, such as insurance and financial services), and imported goods and services worth nearly $3 trillion. One assessment suggests that U.S. consumers get 25 percent more buying power through international trade today, relative to a world with no trade. Inflation-adjusted U.S. exports have grown half again as fast as total U.S. GDP since World War II. The reductions of U.S. tariffs since World War II are estimated to have added roughly $10,000 per year per U.S. household in additional purchasing power.[155]

There is room for more progress. America has prospered as the world's economies increasingly have become interconnected. Industry value chains stretch across nations today. Production crisscrosses borders, as components are both imported and exported to assemble products into final goods.[156] Capital flows from nation to nation, as does direct investment, and cities around the world have become home to the expatriated employees of multi-national companies. As just one vivid indicator of the increasing openness of the world economy, foreign direct investment globally has increased by a factor of almost 42 in real dollars from 1970 to 2015—or about eight times as fast as world GDP.[157] These trends have strengthened the U.S. economy, enhanced U.S. security, and supported U.S. diplomacy around the world.

But while trade growth has been both enormous and rapid, it has also been patchy. Trade barriers have fallen and markets have been liberalized around the world, particularly since the fall of communism and the rise of emerging markets. But many barriers to trade remain. While nearly 70 percent of the world's exports enter U.S. markets duty free, U.S. producers face an average 6.8 percent tariff for their exports. And businesses in many sectors must grapple with other market barriers, quotas, weak intellectual property protections, and other restrictions.[158] By one index of economic globalization, the United States has fallen in relative standing among the "most globalized" nations over the past few decades, not because actual economic flows have fallen but because its policies have not kept pace with the rest of the world. Other countries' restrictions in the form of import barriers, tariffs and tax rates, and capital controls have fallen dramatically relative to those in the United States.[159]

Open trade must be the cornerstone of U.S. trade policy. Prosperity can grow broadly and capitalism can be made stronger if the global integration of trade, production, capital, and talent are strengthened—and the global playing field is more aggressively leveled. Business and policy leaders should continue to seek to *reduce* barriers to trade in every market in the world. Some believe the deck is stacked against U.S. exports; but refusing to negotiate obviously will not solve that problem. The solution is not to import less, but to export more.

The United States should lead the world in lowering tariffs and reducing other barriers to market access in agricultural products, particularly from developing world nations. This includes de-linking agricultural subsidies from prices and production. Emblematic of the flaws in U.S. agricultural policy are incentives that encourage overproduction at public expense, while impoverishing the very nations U.S. businesses see as their growth markets.

The United States should embrace the Trans-Pacific Partnership. The United States also should seek to eliminate all tariffs and quotas in manufactured goods, without exception, in all markets, worldwide, and seek greater liberalization of trade in services.

PROMOTE ADJUSTMENT POLICIES, NOT TRADE PROTECTIONS

Trading nations should capitalize on all of this progress. Anti-dumping and countervailing duty remedies to offset the competitive dynamics of trade are counterproductive. Trading systems must be open. The United States should lead the world in setting an agenda for adjustments—proactive policies that offer workers and communities hope for the future—as opposed to protections that only delay needed and inevitable economic transitions.

Capitalism would be enriched if policymakers stopped trying to ease the human impact of global competition by managing markets and sectors, and instead focused on workers and their communities. Policies oriented to adjustment should seek to cushion the blow to people from the dislocations brought about by globalization and technological change. These policies should also help workers and communities transition to new roles within the economy, rather than try to preserve existing jobs artificially by protecting them from forces of change. Creative destruction must be allowed to drive the economy forward, but public policy must ensure that human capital is re-allocated into new productive uses as an essential part of that process—to function as a "shock absorber" for difficult but unavoidable change.

That underscores the need for flexible adjustment policies that encourage and facilitate worker re-employment. The United States must commit to forging an aggressive, systematic, and effective adjustment system. America's track record in this area has been poor. Job losses in select sectors of the U.S. economy over the last 20 years demonstrate that some displaced workers lack the skills or the training to easily re-enter the workforce, and worker incentives to take steps to do so are stunted. But differing political agendas through the years have created many incremental programs, the sum of whose efforts has been half-hearted, fragmented, and costly. By rationalizing and integrating these programs, and by eliminating various trade-distorting subsidy programs, the plight of displaced workers could be addressed more effectively and affordably. Business leaders should press for a national policy of economic adjustment, going beyond the current Trade Adjustment Assistance (TAA) system,[160] which would be available to all workers experiencing involuntary unemployment for reasons other than their own conduct. Whenever possible, such a program would create incentives for getting back to work.

CED's recommendations include:

- "Wage insurance," which would pay workers a fraction of any income loss associated with a new job, regardless of the reason for the job loss, for a two-year period following the initial job loss. A health insurance supplement could be included. Workers therefore would have a strong incentive to go back to work. Such benefits are now available under restricted circumstances; we would make the program universal. A variation on this theme would be the establishment of an account that an unemployed worker could draw upon, with a proviso that, upon accepting a new job, the worker would have immediate access to the balance of the account as a bonus.

- Additional training should be available to willing workers displaced for any reason. The wage insurance proposal above would encourage workers to accept jobs that hold the prospect of valuable on-the-job-training that could lead to subsequent advancement.

- Job-search assistance should be available. For many workers who are displaced after an extended period of time on a single job, help in searching for new work could prove highly valuable. It might also be especially useful for workers who might need to relocate a significant distance from their old jobs.

REFORM IMMIGRATION POLICY

Two opposing views on the economic impact of immigration dominate American public opinion today. Immigration opponents believe that "outsiders" are displacing Americans from jobs, either because immigrants (often referring to legal immigrants) have the skills (or gain them in U.S. universities) to compete with and replace native-born workers, or because immigrants have few skills and little education (often particularly referring to undocumented immigrants), and thus receive greater value (in welfare, social, and education benefits) than they contribute to the economy. By contrast, immigration supporters contend that immigrants (whether legal or illegal) merely *add* labor supply to the economy and do not crowd out any native-born employment, and hence are a large unambiguous net positive.

These extreme views are oversimplifications, as extreme views tend to be. Immigrant workers are neither perfect complements to, nor perfect substitutes for, native-born workers. The United States has experienced a historic wave of immigration since the mid-1960s (immigrants and their descendants drove more than half of all population growth in the United States during the last five decades), and the economic impact of this influx has been a net positive.[161] But immigration has also triggered frictions that come with competition. Immigrants have competed directly with native-born workers in both low-skill (for example, service) and high-skill (technology) sectors, and sometimes win those jobs. But often immigrant workers accept jobs that native-born workers would not accept. And studies show that displaced native-born workers in many developed economies, including the United States, frequently transition to other jobs in the same sector (sometimes higher paying), or to other sectors. They rarely are doomed to unemployment. (Over much of the period since the financial crisis, when unemployment has been extraordinarily high, the net flow of at least Mexican migration with the United States has reversed.[162])

There's another way in which immigration has benefited the U.S. economy. Competition between immigrant and native-born workers has furthered the occupational specialization that has made the entire U.S. workforce more efficient and productive. Immigrant workers coming from other countries, and often having been educated in different cultures and different languages, tend to bring different "comparative advantages" that can "complement" experienced native-born workers. As economists on both sides of the political spectrum have long argued, the availability of resources (such as different kinds of labor) that work well together strengthens the economy. And many immigrants launch new businesses to optimize delivery of those niche goods or services or to serve the growing needs of employed immigrants. New waves of immigrants increasingly bring significant human capital to the economy, so they are more likely to earn higher income, pay higher taxes, and have less need for government benefits.[163]

U.S. immigration policy should be reformed to maximize these economic benefits. Currently, the system for allocating visas is designed to police arbitrary quantity constraints to types of visas by country of origin. Instead, visas should be allocated to drive an increase of immigrant supply to those occupations that are in greatest shortage. A recent report by The Conference Board shows that many of the greatest shortages in talent—in sectors such as health care, mathematics, and in skilled trades—cannot be met by the supply of native-born workers alone over the next 10 to 15 years.[164] Nations that currently supply the United States with the largest numbers of qualified immigrants for those occupations are severely oversubscribed against their limits for permanent employment-based visas, and have long waiting lists. Meanwhile, temporary employment visas such as the H-1B visa have overall (not country-specific) caps that are reached routinely within the first few days of the annual application period. Another problem with U.S. visa policy is that the criteria to qualify for an employment-based visa are almost entirely based on higher-education attainment (bachelor's and graduate-level degrees), and the employment-based visa categories do not distinguish among the many different types of occupations and thus are incapable of steering immigrants into high-shortage occupations.

One model for "smarter" immigration policy is Canada, which sets visa eligibility based on six factors that rate visa applicants on their adaptability and potential to be productive contributors to the Canadian labor force. This point system utilizes both quantitative and qualitative measures to assess visa applicants, looking at factors such as education, language proficiency, and age. (Visa applicants must take a language test and have proof of current and/or past employment; their educational history and background is scrutinized, including having their educational credits measured against Canadian standards.) Canada invites only the visa candidates who rank the highest in these measures to apply to immigrate.

COORDINATE MULTILATERAL INTERNATIONAL GOVERNANCE ON GLOBALIZATION

A highly globalized, interdependent economy requires high levels of communication, cooperation, and coordination among all participants in order to maximize the shared and combined economic benefits. International organizations such as the World Trade Organization (WTO), the International Monetary Fund (IMF), the Organization for Economic Cooperation and Development (OECD), and the World Bank play critical roles as institutions for coordination. The World Trade Organization, for instance, is a mechanism for promoting trade and for settling trade disputes, while the International Monetary Fund focuses on safeguarding global financial systems.

Business and policy leaders should support these and other institutions that could help contribute to the smooth workings of global capitalism. These leaders also should encourage global institutions and other global platforms to focus on continuing to press all nations to make their borders more open to the flow of workers, goods, services, and investment. Coordination among nations should seek to keep playing fields level, and to ensure economic signals are clear and undistorted, so that resources can move to their highest-valued uses. International coordination of government policies is needed beyond trade policy, as well, to further economic growth. For example, differences in tax policies across countries unintentionally and counterproductively can tilt the global playing field.

The protection of intellectual property (IP) within multilateral trade agreements typically is weak. A balance must be struck between establishing strong IP protections that encourage innovation (via adequate rewards to the original creators of ideas), yet are not so restrictive as to stifle competition among businesses and the spread of new ideas and their benefits to the economy and society more broadly. The establishment of the World Trade Organization (WTO) in 1995 resulted in the inclusion of IP rights issues within the rules-based multilateral trade system. The WTO agreement on "Trade Related Aspects of IP Rights" (or TRIPs) imposes minimum standards covering the 153 member countries.

■ ■ ■

"Protection is the dog that did not bark," observed *Financial Times* columnist Martin Wolf in 2013.[165] National capitalism effectively has given way to global capitalism and trade, and attempts by anti-globalist forces in many nations to reverse course since the 2008 downturn generally have failed. The current of history—of economic progress—is against them.

But Wolf added that proponents of globalization should not be complacent. Within developed economies, the legacy of unequal distribution of the benefits of globalization is stirring a public backlash. The stunning decision by British voters to leave the European Union, the growing populist anger gathering on both the right and the left flanks of U.S. politics, and the rise of nationalism elsewhere in Europe, are warning signs to business and policy leaders everywhere that failure to make the benefits of capitalism inclusive has gone on far too long. Capitalism will suffer if this failure continues.

Business leaders own this challenge to make capitalism's benefits more inclusive, even if most of the needed solutions are policy reforms. They own it because the challenge is primarily economic, and policy reforms must unleash market forces, not constrain them. Economic vision must guide the social investments America urgently needs to make. Business leaders should be stewards not only of their businesses today, but also of the businesses—and the economy—of tomorrow.

Business leaders must not shirk their responsibility to make capitalism sustainable for the twenty-first century. The future of the entire U.S. economy—businesses and families alike—depends on their leadership. Promoting truly free trade, using adjustment policies to help those who lose ground because of change, creating and implementing sound immigration policy, and reaching to other nations to make capitalism sustainable globally are the highest priorities.

CONCLUSION

The Path Forward to Renewed Prosperity

WE WROTE THIS BOOK for a simple reason: We want to see a return to the long-term growth trajectory that made the United States the most prosperous nation in the world. But as we survey the economic and political landscape, we see troubling indicators that suggest the principles underpinning our prosperity are fraying: plunging trust in business, diminished confidence in the fairness of our economic system, and a loss of faith in capitalism itself. Unless these sentiments change, the dynamism that's been a defining feature of the U.S. economy for decades will be displaced by stagnation and sclerosis.

Despite capitalism's achievements throughout our nation's history, changes in technology and in the world economy leave a never-ending challenge to keep our economy at the cutting edge, meeting the needs of our people. That is a challenge for institutions and individuals representing all interests and ideologies—but it is a special challenge for business leaders.

They are on the frontlines of the economy—providing the goods and services that power the U.S. economy, and paychecks for millions of people. Business leaders know from experience what builds prosperity and, just as important, what doesn't. And they know that to ensure the broadest possible success, businesses need a public-policy and regulatory environment that supports expanding opportunity and enterprise. Regrettably, many of today's policies and regulations are handicapping businesses as they strive to compete at home and abroad. Reforming policy and regulation is difficult precisely because of the widespread loss of faith in U.S. public institutions and the U.S. capitalist system.

The preceding chapters presented comprehensive reforms that would revitalize the economy and generate renewed prosperity, but just as importantly would lay the groundwork for renewed public trust and therefore capitalism's sustainability. The list may seem long, but it is no more than the nation has achieved in the past when citizens and business patriots came together with a shared purpose and devotion to the common good. Business must demonstrate its commitment to transparency and accountability, and show that we are all in this together. The processes of Washington must be reformed to facilitate action through honorable compromise. And the resulting policy action must end the fundamental threats to our economic system posed by fiscal irresponsibility, the unsustainably growing cost of some essential public programs, the lagging development of our workforce skills, and regulatory and global roadblocks to growth. All of these reforms are essential to sustaining capitalism for the benefit of all Americans. What follows is a summary of many of those proposed reforms.

PROMOTE COMPETITION, COMBAT CRONY CAPITALISM

First and most fundamentally, business must demonstrate its commitment to competition on a fair basis, and for all. Too many Americans have come to believe that the U.S. economy is rigged in favor of those who have through various means acquired the favor of government officials. This sentiment, which breeds cynicism and distrust, is not without some justification: as government has taken on a greater role within the economy, the potential rewards for influencing public policy have grown. And while crony capitalism has tarnished the reputation of business, the vast majority of businesses compete on a level playing field, where everyone abides by the same rules.

To change the terms of the debate on cronyism, business leaders need to speak to their fellow citizens, and their elected policymakers, about how business is and should be done and why cronyism is a corrosive force within the economy. These business leaders also need to practice the gospel of fair competition that they preach. In turn, our elected policymakers should resist deals that smack of cronyism and seek to reverse those that already exist. And they should be rewarded by the voters for doing so.

COUNTER SHORT-TERMISM

Again, to establish its credibility, business must first tend to its own house. One of the threats to capitalism's sustainability arising from business itself is an excessive focus on short-term results among owners (shareholders in the case of corporations), boards, and executives. This focus comes at the expense of longer-term value and results. To counter short-termism, corporate leaders—both executives and boards of directors—should communicate to all concerned—including the general public—their objectives and time horizons. Executive compensation should be tied to these objective and time horizons, with transparency and accountability. Firms should also choose a multi-stakeholder approach to value creation and aim for maintenance of value over the long term. Adopting a long-term perspective leads directly to a multi-stakeholder approach, because companies cannot prosper over the long run without also achieving the success and sustainability of their customers, employees, suppliers, the environment, and the communities in which they do business.

IMPROVE THE NATION'S FISCAL HEALTH

One of the truly critical issues that Congress and the President have failed to adequately address is the persistence of large budget deficits and continued growth of the federal debt. This fiscal irresponsibility threatens the very stability of the U.S. economy and U.S. leadership around the world. It must be remedied, through early action with gradual and measured but predictable results. Key priorities are described in the following section.

Subject Medicare to Market Forces

Medicare is enormously important to millions of America's seniors, but it is also the largest contributor to the projected future growth of the public debt. If that cost growth is not remedied, our seniors will lose their access to quality care that they can afford. Rather than try to use government-appointed boards to drive down costs, government and business should work together to unleash market forces. The nation's senior citizens should be able to choose from among traditional Medicare and many private plans competing with it according to the same rules to provide quality, affordable care. This will drive down Medicare's program cost for taxpayers and seniors themselves while improving the quality of care through a choice of delivery systems meeting seniors' diverse preferences.

Review Discretionary Spending

Congress should undertake a regular, systematic analysis of each area of domestic discretionary spending to identify those programs that deserve reauthorization and those that require changes to be made more efficient. Such periodic reviews will improve the effectiveness and accountability of government. Defense spending also should be scrutinized through the same careful process, to attain all possible efficiencies and savings and an even greater national security. Where appropriate, public-private partnerships can increase financing for important productivity-increasing public investments.

Strengthen Social Security

Social Security's financing should not be approached from the vantage point of deficit reduction but rather with the goal of securing and strengthening a critical foundation for the retirement for future generations. Both parties in Congress should work together with the President to adjust benefits and enhance revenues to set the program back on sound financial footing. Needed reforms include gradually raising the maximum earned income subject to the payroll tax to cover 90 percent of all wages (and maintain that share in later years), using a more accurate calculation of annual cost of living adjustments, while adjusting benefits for increasing life expectancies, implementing modest additional means testing for high-income beneficiaries, and restoring protections for workers who earn low wages and who have interrupted careers.

Reform the Tax Code

Tax reform is central to sustaining capitalism. It can contribute to fairness and trust among all citizens; it can speed economic growth, and the growth of incomes; and it can reduce the federal budget deficit and the now-burgeoning debt burden. The tax code needs to be streamlined to achieve greater simplicity while also leveling the economic playing field. Business leaders should press the congressional tax-writing committees to build broad, bipartisan support for comprehensive reform. We endorse a specific and innovative tax reform plan that would replace and restructure the low-income relief provisions for working families and the current system of itemized deductions, eliminate most tax preferences for particular forms of income or spending, and reduce and simplify tax rates for both individuals and corporations.

REFORM HEALTH CARE

The rising cost of health care is inflating government, business, and household budgets. One of the keys to making quality care and universal access compatible with affordable costs is greater consumer choice, which would drive plans and providers to seek greater efficiency and lower costs, while providing the quality that consumers want. This would require real choices among a variety of competing insurance plans. One size does not fit all: consumers have different preferences for care depending on their needs and where they live, and want products that meet their individual expectations.

At the same time, government intervention in health care must be curtailed. The federal government must limit its role to setting standards of coverage and care quality, enforcing sound consumer protections, and ensuring the playing field is fair, to prevent a "race to the bottom" dynamic. Government also should resist trying to protect the status quo. The diversity of plans that will appear, aimed at meeting consumer needs, will disrupt traditional plan and provider models. This is essential to increase quality and slow the growth of costs, just as it does in all other industries. In particular, the perverse fee-for-service model dominant in health care today will come under fire in a competitive market. Fee-for-service health care shackles competition and process improvement, and encourages overuse and waste—inefficiencies that are competed away in more open markets.

IMPROVE EDUCATION

Today's young Americans are falling behind their counterparts in our competitor nations in both knowledge and degree completion. Similarly, workers are not keeping up with skill needs, and are tripping over transitions from obsolete to cutting-edge jobs. This is a trajectory toward decline and decay. The quality of our workforce will be key to sustaining capitalism.

Among the many possible solutions, three categories stand out. First, there should be additional investment and attention to early care and education of children ages 0–5, because early learning sets the foundation for developing our nation's human capital. Research findings consistently have shown a high return on investment for high-quality programs serving disadvantaged children. Second, significant reform to the United States K12 public education system is needed, with a focus on concerted and systematic improvement in boosting student readiness, improved teacher quality, and raising the bar on the quality of *what* is taught. Third, national goals for post-secondary education and workforce development need to be rethought, with the primary focus on education's role in preparing students for employment.

REFORM CAMPAIGN FINANCE

The money chase in today's campaign finance system is corrosive to the public trust in government. We need campaign finance reform to free elected officials from their dependence on the continuous cycle of private campaign funding, and thereby to restore public faith in our democratic political system. One way would be to empower small-dollar campaign contributions, with government matching the first $250 of every campaign donation, perhaps by a multiple of as much as four to one. This would make small donations more valuable to a campaign, which might induce candidates to put more effort into pursuing small donations, and into connecting with a greater number of voters. It might also allow candidates to achieve a competitive level of finance solely through benign small contributions, the sheer numbers of which would make exploiting them to influence candidates for personal gain either highly unlikely or impossible.

END JUDICIAL ELECTIONS

While federal judges are nominated by the President, there are 39 states that use elections to choose their judges. That means campaigning for office and raising campaign contributions, which can lead to unseemly campaigns and incentives for judges and interest groups to weigh contributions on a political balance. An appointment system for state-level judges would be far superior, with nonpartisan commissions selecting judges based on merit. Such commissions recruit and recommend eligible nominees for judicial appointments. The commission's independence can be strengthened by dispersing power to appoint members of the commission across a variety of offices, including the governor and legislators from both parties.

REFORM LOBBYING

In tandem with campaign finance reform, the lobbying reform should reduce special interest leverage over the legislative process. There should be tighter restrictions on members of Congress and their staffs seeking employment in lobbying firms upon leaving Capitol Hill. The so-called "cooling-off" period before a member who leaves the House may engage in any form of lobbying should be extended to two years (this rule already applies in the Senate). The same restrictions could apply to employees of government agencies or regulatory authorities. Another valuable reform would be to ban any registered lobbyist, and any institution that hires registered lobbyists, from raising or soliciting contributions for federal candidates and officeholders. They should not be allowed, either, to serve as treasurers of Leadership PACs and other campaign fundraising organizations.

Just as important is strengthening enforcement of laws and ethics rules that cover members of Congress, staff, and lobbyists. Given that the committees with ethics responsibilities have not fulfilled their responsibilities, it may be time to establish a strong and independent enforcement authority to help Congress punish and deter ethical violations by lobbyists and members. A nonpartisan ethics enforcement authority, perhaps within the Government Accountability Office, could be composed of distinguished former members of Congress and retired judges, insulated from political pressure.

OVERHAUL THE REDISTRICTING PROCESS

The process used to draw the districts for the House of Representatives and state legislatures needs a sweeping overhaul. Federal action would be welcome, but failing that, states should use their authority over the electoral process to reform their own redistricting institutions. One option would be the appointment of nonpartisan commissions in each state, with a focus on creating districts that are equal in population, compact, contiguous, and competitive (that is, approximately equally divided by party affiliation), in that order of priority.

FIX THE CONGRESSIONAL POLICYMAKING PROCESS

The U.S. policymaking process is riddled with shortcomings, and many of the longstanding rules and procedures of the legislative process have been abused by the leadership of both parties. The net effect is shortsighted policies and declining public trust in the fairness of the policy-making process. The following procedural reforms are needed:

- The House should limit the use of closed rules (which typically restrict the time allowed for debate and the numbers of amendments) to truly urgent pieces of legislation. Enacting this reform would allow for more deliberation and expression of a variety of views during debate.

- The House and the Senate should appoint promptly members to conference committees, including members from the minority party. These appointments should include those who have drafted the legislation.

- Congress (especially the House) should change its schedule to comprise at least two-week periods of Monday-through-Friday sessions, with weeks off in between to allow time in the home districts. Such a schedule would allow more time for oversight and substantive hearings, while helping to foster personal relationships which contribute to constructive compromise.

- The House should use self-executing rules, which change bills passed by committees of jurisdiction before they go to the House floor, only in instances of true emergencies, or where revisions of bills are purely in the nature of technical correction rather than substantive alteration.

- The Senate "hold" should be cut back to its former purpose of allowing Senators to exercise their judgment on nominations from their states only.

- Congress should rededicate itself to timely appropriations. Delays and uncertainty in funding waste taxpayer dollars, and render government less effective and efficient. Appropriations bills should be debated individually and in the open.

- Congress should reenact budget disciplines—spending caps for annual appropriations, and pay-as-you-go requirements for entitlement spending and taxes—that worked in the 1990s.

BRING GREATER EFFICIENCY TO THE REGULATORY PROCESS

The process of writing federal and state regulations often results in favoritism for politically powerful incumbent businesses—to the detriment of new business formation and the innovation and productivity growth of the overall economy. When developing any new regulation, there needs to be more focus on the public interest justification and the goals or principles that are intended to be served. And those goals and principles should be defined so they can be measured and so that regulations can be designed, maintained, monitored—and periodically updated, as necessary. The entire government regulatory process also should be more open and transparent. By making the regulatory drafting and review process more inclusive, regulations (and government in general) will be more impartial and more supportive of the public interest (and less supportive of crony capitalism).

INTEGRATE WITH THE GLOBAL ECONOMY AND EXPAND ADJUSTMENT POLICIES

Policies that erect barriers to imports (or penalize companies for producing globally) will disadvantage all Americans, and impair American prosperity. The answer is not to retreat but to move forward, with open trade the cornerstone of U.S. trade policy. Prosperity can grow broadly and capitalism can be made stronger if the global integration of trade, production, capital, and talent are strengthened—and the global playing field is more aggressively leveled. Business and policy leaders should continue to seek to *reduce* barriers to trade in every market in the world.

It's also critically important to balance the ledger of globalization, with a focus on policies and programs that support workers and communities caught in the transitions inherent in globalization, while spreading the gains of globalization more widely. Policies oriented to adjustment should seek to cushion the blow from the dislocations brought about by globalization and technological change. These policies should also help workers and communities transition to new roles within the economy, rather than try to preserve existing jobs artificially by protecting them from forces of change. Key recommendations include:

- Congress should approve a more universal "wage insurance," which would reimburse workers for a fraction of any income loss associated with taking a new lower-paying job (regardless of the reason for the job loss), for a two-year period following the initial job loss. A health insurance supplement could be included. Expanding wage insurance would give workers a strong incentive to accept new employment rather than settling for extended unemployment compensation.

- Additional training should be available to willing workers displaced for any reason, perhaps as a condition for eligibility for extended unemployment benefits. The wage insurance proposal above would encourage workers to accept jobs that hold the prospect of valuable on-the-job-training that could lead to subsequent advancement.

- Job-search assistance should be available. For many workers who are displaced after an extended period of time on a single job, help in searching for new work could prove highly valuable. It might also be especially useful for workers who might need to relocate a significant distance from their old jobs.

REFORM IMMIGRATION POLICY

The United States has experienced a historic wave of immigration since the mid-1960s and the economic impact of this influx has been a net positive. But immigration also has triggered frictions that come with competition. Immigrants have competed directly with native-born workers in both low-skill and high-skill sectors. This competition has helped make the entire U.S. workforce more efficient and productive, as well as larger. Many immigrants also launch new businesses to optimize delivery of niche goods or services or to serve the growing needs of employed immigrants. And because new waves of immigrants increasingly bring significant human capital to the economy, those new workers are more likely to earn higher income, pay higher taxes, and have less need for government benefits.

U.S. immigration policy should be reformed to maximize these economic benefits. Currently, the system for allocating visas is designed to police arbitrary quantity constraints on types of visas by country of origin. Instead, visas should be allocated to drive an increase of immigrant supply to those occupations that are in greatest shortage.

One model for "smarter" immigration policy is Canada, which sets visa eligibility based on six factors that rate visa applicants on their adaptability and potential to be productive contributors to the Canadian labor force. This point system utilizes both quantitative and qualitative measures to assess visa applicants, looking at factors such as education, language proficiency, and age.

PROMOTE MORE EFFECTIVE INTERNATIONAL GOVERNANCE

A highly integrated and interdependent global economy requires high levels of communication, cooperation, and coordination among all participants in order to maximize the shared and combined economic benefits. International organizations such as the World Trade Organization (WTO), the International Monetary Fund (IMF), the Organization for Economic Cooperation and Development (OECD), and the World Bank play critical roles as institutions for coordination. Business and policy leaders should support these and other institutions that could help contribute to the smooth workings of global capitalism. These leaders also should encourage global institutions and other global platforms to focus on continuing to press all nations to make their borders more open to the flow of workers, goods, services, and investment.

THE IMPERATIVE OF BUSINESS LEADERSHIP

While the vast majority of these proposed reforms are for policymakers to enact, the nation's elected officials have not acted on their own. Business leaders must step forward. By entering the public square, and speaking out for change, they can help policymakers—and the broader public—understand precisely why these reforms are needed. Business leaders can emphasize how the reforms will contribute to greater long-term prosperity for all Americans—and thereby make capitalism more sustainable—through first-hand knowledge of how the benefits to the nation flow through their own day-to-day operations.

We seek the commitment of the entire U.S. business community—from all parts of the country, and spanning all industries—to take this agenda to our elected policymakers, and to begin a respectful public debate on these issues. Seventy-five years ago, leadership from the American business community helped lay the foundation for policies that made the United States the most prosperous nation in the world. That leadership is needed again.

DETAILED CED
POLICY STATEMENTS

The following CED policy statements provide greater detail on our assessments of the key issues identified in each chapter of this book, and our recommendations for public and business policy.

1. The Structural Threats to Capitalism—And the Structure of a Solution

Tackling Economic Inequality, Boosting Opportunity: A Blueprint for Business (Arlington, VA: Committee for Economic Development, April 6, 2016), www.ced .org/pdf/CED-Inequality-Report.pdf.

Leadership and Shared Purpose for America's Future (Washington, D.C.: Committee for Economic Development, October 22, 2008), www.ced.org/reports/single/ leadership-and-shared-purpose-for-americas-future.

2. Crony Capitalism

Crony Capitalism: Unhealthy Relations Between Business and Government (Arlington, VA: Committee for Economic Development, October 14, 2015), www.ced.org/pdf/ CED_-_Crony_Capitalism_-_Report.pdf.

Ben W. Heineman Jr., *Restoring Trust in Corporate Governance: The Six Essential Tasks of Boards of Directors and Business Leaders* (Washington, D.C.: Committee for Economic Development, January 25, 2010), www.ced.org/reports/single/ restoring-trust-in-corporate-governance.

Private Enterprise, Public Trust: The State of Corporate America After Sarbanes-Oxley (Washington, D.C.: Committee for Economic Development, March 21, 2006), www.ced.org/reports/single/private-enterprise-public-trust-the-state-of-corporate-america-after-s.

3. Focusing on Long-Term Value: Reversing Business Short-Termism

Every Other One: More Women on Corporate Boards (Washington, D.C.: Committee for Economic Development, November 13, 2014), www.ced.org/reports/single/ every-other-one-more-women-on-corporate-boards.

Business Statesmanship and Sustainable Capitalism: Can Corporate Leaders Help Put America and American Business Back on Track? (Washington, D.C.: Committee for Economic Development, May 28, 2013), www.ced.org/pdf/Business_Statesman_Working_Paper_Final.pdf.

Fulfilling the Promise: How More Women on Corporate Boards Would Make America and American Companies More Competitive (Washington, D.C.: Committee for Economic Development, June 26, 2012), www.ced.org/reports/single/fulfilling-the-promise.

Ben W. Heineman, Jr. and Stephen Davis, *Are Institutional Investors Part of the Problem or Part of the Solution?* (Washington, D.C.: Committee for Economic Development, October 3, 2011), www.ced.org/reports/single/are-institutional-investors-part-of-the-problem-or-part-of-the-solution.

Rebuilding Corporate Leadership: How Directors Can Link Long-Term Performance with Public Goals (Washington, D.C.: Committee for Economic Development, February 18, 2009), www.ced.org/reports/single/rebuilding-corporate-leadership-how-directors-can-link-long-term-perfo.

Built to Last: Focusing Corporations on Long-Term Performance (Washington, D.C.: Committee for Economic Development, June 27, 2007), www.ced.org/reports/single/built-to-last-focusing-corporations-on-long-term-performance.

4. Reform Education

Child Care in State Economies (Arlington, VA: Committee for Economic Development, August 1, 2015), www.ced.org/childcareimpact.

The Role of Business in Promoting Education Attainment: A National Imperative (Arlington, VA: Committee for Economic Development, April 22, 2015), www.ced.org/pdf/20150714_Lumina.pdf.

How Business Leaders Can Support College- and Career-Readiness: Staying the Course on Common Core (Washington, D.C.: Committee for Economic Development, November 12, 2014), www.ced.org/pdf/White_Paper.pdf.

William R. Doyle, *A New Partnership: Reshaping the Federal and State Commitment to Need-Based Aid* (Washington, D.C.: Committee for Economic Development, January 24, 2013), www.ced.org/reports/single/a-new-partnership-the-road-to-reshaping-federal-state-financial-aid.

Unfinished Business: Continued Investment in Child Care and Early Education is Critical to Business and America's Future (Washington, D.C.: Committee for Economic Development, June 26, 2012), www.ced.org/pdf/Unfinished-Business.pdf.

Boosting Postsecondary Education Performance (Washington, D.C.: Committee for Economic Development, April 30, 2012), www.ced.org/reports/single/boosting-postsecondary-education-performance.

Harnessing Openness to Improve Research, Teaching and Learning in Higher Education (Washington, D.C.: Committee for Economic Development, November 5, 2009), www.ced.org/reports/single/harnessing-openness-to-improve-research-teaching-and-learning-in-higher-edu.

Teacher Compensation and Teacher Quality (Washington, D.C.: Committee for Economic Development, October 1, 2009), www.ced.org/reports/single/teacher-compensation-and-teacher-quality.

The Economic Promise of Investing in High-Quality Preschool: Using Early Education to Improve Economic Growth and the Fiscal Sustainability of States and the Nation (Washington, D.C.: Committee for Economic Development, June 26, 2006), www.ced.org/reports/single/the-economic-promise-of-investing-in-high-quality-preschool.

Education for Global Leadership: The Importance of International Studies and foreign Language Education for U.S. Economic and National Security (Washington, D.C.: Committee for Economic Development, May 17, 2006), www.ced.org/reports/single/education-for-global-leadership.

Ellen Galinsky, *The Economic Benefits of High-Quality Early Childhood Programs: What Makes the Difference?* (Washington, D.C.: Committee for Economic Development, February 15, 2006), www.ced.org/reports/single/the-economic-benefits-of-high-quality-early-childhood-programs-what-makes-t.

Cracks in the Education Pipeline: A Business Leader's Guide to Higher Education Reform (Washington, D.C.: Committee for Economic Development, June 14, 2005), www.ced.org/reports/single/cracks-in-the-education-pipeline-a-business-leaders-guide-to-higher-educati.

5. Making Washington Work

Making Washington Work (Arlington, VA.: Committee for Economic Development, forthcoming 2017).

Choosing Justice? The Need for Judicial Selection Reform (Arlington, VA: Committee for Economic Development, November 18, 2015), www.ced.org/reports/single/choosing-justice-the-need-for-judicial-selection-reform.

Anthony Corrado, *Hiding in Plain Sight: The Problem of Transparency in Political Finance* (Washington, D.C.: Committee for Economic Development, July 24, 2013), www.ced.org/reports/single/hiding-in-plain-sight-the-problem-of-transparency-in-political-finance.

After Citizens United: Improving Accountability in Political Finance (Washington, D.C.: Committee for Economic Development, September 26, 2011), www.ced.org/pdf/After-Citizens-United.pdf.

Hidden Money: The Need for Transparency in Political Finance (Washington, D.C.: Committee for Economic Development, September 26, 2011), www.ced.org/reports/single/hidden-money-the-need-for-transparency-in-political-finance.

Partial Justice: The Peril of Judicial Elections (Washington, D.C.: Committee for Economic Development, September 26, 2011), www.ced.org/reports/single/partial-justice-hidden-money-and-after-citizens-united.

Building on Reform: A Business Proposal to Strengthen Election Finance (Washington, D.C.: Committee for Economic Development, April 5, 2005), www.ced.org/reports/single/building-on-reform-a-business-proposal-to-strengthen-campaign-finance.

6. A Prescription for Fiscal Health

Policy Statement on Fiscal Health (Arlington, VA: Committee for Economic Development, forthcoming, November 2016).

Modernizing Medicare (Arlington, VA: Committee for Economic Development, October 19, 2016), www.ced.org/reports/single/modernizing-medicare.

Adjusting the Prescription: CED Recommendations for Health Care Reform (Arlington, VA: Committee for Economic Development, (April 23, 2015), www.ced.org/reports/single/adjusting-the-prescription-ced-recommendations-for-health-care-reform.

Alain C. Enthoven, *To Reform Medicare, Reform Incentives and Organization* (Washington, D.C.: Committee for Economic Development, November 4, 2011), www.ced.org/reports/single/to-reform-medicare-reform-incentives-and-organization.

This Way Down—To a Debt Crisis (Washington, D.C.: Committee for Economic Development, January 25, 2011), www.ced.org/reports/single/this-way-down-to-a-debt-crisis.

Harnessing Openness to Transform America's Health Care (Washington, D.C.: Committee for Economic Development, December 19, 2008), www.ced.org/reports/single/harnessing-openness-to-transform-american-health-care.

Quality, Affordable Health Care for All: Moving Beyond the Employer-Based Health-Insurance System (Washington, D.C.: Committee for Economic Development, November 14, 2007), www.ced.org/reports/single/quality-affordable-health-care-for-all-moving-beyond-the-employer-base.

The Employer-based Health-Insurance System (EBI) Is At Risk: What We Must Do About It (Washington, D.C.: Committee for Economic Development, July 17, 2007), www.ced.org/reports/single/the-employer-based-health-insurance-system-ebi-is-at-risk-what-we-must-do-a.

A New Tax Framework: A Blueprint for Averting a Fiscal Crisis (Washington, D.C.: Committee for Economic Development, September 23, 2005), www.ced.org/reports/single/a-new-tax-framework-a-blueprint-for-averting-a-fiscal-crisis.

Fixing Social Security: A CED Policy Update (Washington, D.C.: Committee for Economic Development, May 18, 2005), www.ced.org/reports/single/fixing-social-security-a-ced-policy-update.

The Emerging Budget Crisis: Urgent Fiscal Choices (Washington, D.C.: Committee for Economic Development, May 13, 2005), www.ced.org/reports/single/the-emerging-budget-crisis-urgent-fiscal-choices.

7. Regulation to Build Trust in Capitalism

Policy Statement on Regulation (Arlington, VA: Committee for Economic Development, forthcoming 2017).

8. Sustainable Capitalism and the Global Economy

Policy Statement on Globalization (Arlington, VA: Committee for Economic Development, forthcoming 2017).

In Support of International Trade: Business Leaders Speak Out (Washington, D.C.: Committee for Economic Development, October 7, 2009), www.ced.org/reports/single/in-support-of-international-trade-business-leaders-speak-out.

Reducing Risks from Global Imbalances (Washington, D.C.: Committee for Economic Development, September 7, 2007), www.ced.org/reports/single/reducing-risks-from-global-imbalances.

Public-Private Partnerships for Development: A Handbook for Business (Washington, D.C.: Committee for Economic Development, July 19, 2006), www.ced.org/reports/single/public-private-partnerships-for-development-a-handbook-for-business.

Reducing Global Poverty: Encouraging Private Investment in Infrastructure (Washington, D.C.: Committee for Economic Development, July 19, 2006), www.ced.org/reports/single/reducing-global-poverty-encouraging-private-investment-in-infrastructure.

Making Trade Work: Straight Talk on Jobs, Trade, and Adjustments (Washington, D.C.: Committee for Economic Development, June 1, 2005), www.ced.org/reports/single/making-trade-work-straight-talk-on-jobs-trade-and-adjustment.

NOTES

1. Sarah Kendzior, "Why Young Americans Are Giving Up on Capitalism," *Foreign Policy*, June 16, 2016, http://foreignpolicy.com/2016/06/16/why-young-americans-are-giving-up-on-capitalism/.

2. "Trust in government: 1958–2015," in *Beyond Distrust: How Americans View Their Government* (Washington, D.C.: Pew Research Center, November 23, 2015), www.people-press.org/2015/11/23/1-trust-in-government-1958-2015/.

3. David Brooks, "The Capitalism Debate," *New York Times*, July 17, 2012, www.nytimes.com/2012/07/17/opinion/brooks-more-capitalism-please.html?_r=0.

4. Although the term "sustainable" has environmental connotations today, we use the word in its more traditional business sense, meaning long-term successful duration. We do not directly address environmental sustainability in this volume.

5. Carmen M. Reinhart and Kenneth S. Rogoff have documented that economic downturns caused by severe financial crises tend to yield tepid and protracted economic recoveries. Carmen M. Reinhart and Kenneth S. Rogoff, "Recovery from Financial Crises: Evidence from 100 Episodes," *American Economic Review* 104, no. 5 (May 2014): 50–55, doi:10.1257/aer.104.5.50.

6. Part (but not all) of this growth slowdown is the result of slower growth in the working-age population because of the retirement of the oversized baby-boom generation.

7. It isn't possible here to list the entire bibliography of CED work in this area, but to highlight a few milestones: *Tackling Economic Inequality, Boosting Opportunity* (Arlington, VA: Committee for Economic Development, April 2016), www.ced.org/reports/single/tackling-economic-inequality-boosting-opportunity-a-blueprint-for-business; *Crony Capitalism: Unhealthy Relations Between Business and Government* (Arlington, VA: Committee for Economic Development, July 2016), www.ced.org/reports/single/crony-capitalism-unhealthy-relations-between-business-and-government; *Business Statesmanship and Sustainable Capitalism: Can Corporate Leaders Help Put America and American Business Back on Track?* (Washington, D.C.: Committee for Economic Development, May 2013), www.ced.org/reports/single/business-statesmanship-and-sustainable-capitalism-can-corporate-leaders-hel; *Rebuilding Corporate Leadership: How*

Directors Can Link Long-Term Performance with Public Goals (Washington, D.C.: Committee for Economic Development, February 2009), www.ced .org/reports/single/rebuilding-corporate-leadership-how-directors-can-link-long-term-perfo; *Built to Last: Focusing Corporations on Long-Term Performance* (Washington, D.C.: Committee for Economic Development, June 2007), www.ced.org/reports/single/built-to-last-focusing-corporations-on-long-term-performance; *Private Enterprise, Public Trust: The State of Corporate America After Sarbanes-Oxley* (Washington, D.C.: Committee for Economic Development, March 2006), www.ced.org/reports/single/private-enterprise-public-trust-the-state-of-corporate-america-after-s; *Social Responsibilities of Business Corporations* (New York, NY: Committee for Economic Development, 1971); and William J. Baumol, Rensis Likert, Henry C. Wallich, and John J. McGowan, *A New Rationale for Corporate Social Policy* (New York, NY: Committee for Economic Development, 1970).

8. Although there are numerous sources of data and analysis, we see as particularly persuasive the findings of the Congressional Budget Office, which has focused on a consistent methodology using the same data sources since 1979, under organizational leadership appointed by both political parties. Their findings show consistent increases in inequality using several alternative measures of income. However, these data relate to only income, not wealth, and they provide limited detail on the very high reaches of the income distribution.

9. Facundo Alvaredo, Tony Atkinson, Thomas Piketty, Emmanuel Saez, and Gabriel Zucman, "The Database," WID—The World Wealth and Income Database, accessed 2016, www.wid.world/#.

10. Beth Ann Bovino, Gabriel J. Petek, and John B. Chambers, *How Increasing Income Inequality Is Dampening US Economic Growth* (Standard & Poor's Rating Services, August 5, 2014), www.ncsl.org/Portals/1/Documents/forum/ Forum_2014/Income_Inequality.pdf.

11. Chul-In Lee and Gary Solon, "Trends in Intergenerational Income Mobility," *Review of Economics and Statistics* 91, no. 4 (November, 2009): 766–772, doi:10.1162/rest.91.4.766, www.mitpressjournals.org/doi/abs/10.1162/ rest.91.4.766#.V-6q_PArKUk. The authors examine data from the Panel Study of Income Dynamics, a long running survey tracking 5,000 families.

12. Raj Chetty, Nathaniel Hendren, Patrick Kline, Emmanuel Saez, and Nicholas Turner, "Is the United States Still a Land of Opportunity? Recent Trends in Intergenerational Mobility," *American Economic Review* 104, no. 5 (May 2014): 141–47, doi: 10.1257/aer.104.5.141, www.aeaweb.org/articles?id=10.1257/aer .104.5.141.

13. For example, one study found that students from the highest quartile of

SAT-equivalent scorers, but the lowest socioeconomic quartile, were less likely to graduate from college than students from the highest socioeconomic quartile but the second lowest SAT-equivalent quartile. See Anthony P. Carnevale and Jeff Strohl, "How Increasing College Access Is Increasing Inequality, and What to Do about It," in *Rewarding Strivers: Helping Low-income Students Succeed in College*, ed. Richard D. Kahlenberg (New York: Century Foundation Press, 2010), 158.

14. Jim Tankersley, "Economic Mobility Hasn't Changed in a Half-Century in America, Economists Declare," *Washington Post*, January 23, 2014, www .washingtonpost.com/business/economy/economic-mobility-hasnt-changed-in-a-half-century-in-america-economists-declare/2014/01/22/e845db4a-83a2 -11e3-8099-9181471f7aaf_story.html.

15. James Manyika, "The Future of Work: Five Issues for the Next Economy," *McKinsey & Company*, November 12, 2015, www.mckinsey.com/mgi/overview/ in-the-news/the-future-of-work-five-issues-for-the-next-economy. Those job losses were offset by other job gains; this is a "gross," not a "net," number of job losses.

16. Frank Levy and Richard J. Murnane, *Dancing with Robots: Human Skills for Computerized Work* (Washington, D.C.: Third Way, July 17, 2013), www .thirdway.org/report/dancing-with-robots-human-skills-for-computerized-work.

17. Michael Chui, James Manyika, and Mehdi Miremadi, "Four Fundamentals of Workplace Automation," *McKinsey Quarterly*, November 2015, www .mckinsey.com/business-functions/business-technology/our-insights/four-fundamentals-of-workplace-automation.

18. Prime working age is considered between 25 and 54 years of age.

19. Sam Fleming, "US Low-skill Males Drop Out of Jobs Market," *Financial Times*, June 20, 2016, www.ft.com/cms/s/0/a5d5a8fe-36f5-11e6-a780-b48ed7b6126f.html#axzz4IGSYgb3v; Council of Economic Advisers, *The Long-Term Decline in Prime-Age Male Labor Force Participation* (Washington, D.C.: Executive Office of the President of the United States, June 2016), www.whitehouse.gov/sites/default/files/page/files/20160620_cea_primeage _male_lfp.pdf.

20. *The Rising Cost of Not Going to College* (Washington, D.C.: Pew Research Center, February 11, 2014), www.pewsocialtrends.org/2014/02/11/the-rising-cost-of-not-going-to-college/; "Annual Earning of Young Adults," National Center for Education Statistics, Institute of Education Sciences, May 2016, https://nces.ed.gov/programs/coe/indicator_cba.asp; Mary C. Daly and Leila Bengali, "Is It Still Worth Going to College?," Federal Reserve Bank of San Francisco, May 5, 2014, www.frbsf.org/economic-research/publications/

economic-letter/2014/may/is-college-worth-it-education-tuition-wages/; Brad Hershbein and Melissa S. Kearney, *Major Decisions: What Graduates Earn Over Their Lifetimes* (Washington, D.C.: The Hamilton Project, September 29, 2014), www.hamiltonproject.org/assets/legacy/files/downloads_and_links/Major_Decisions_Lifetime__Earnings_by_Major.pdf.

21. David Weidner, "Hedge Fund Managers' Pay Slashed to $211,538 an Hour," *MarketWatch*, May 5, 2015, www.marketwatch.com/story/hedge-fund-managers-pay-slashed-to-211538-an-hour-2015-05-05; Stephen Taub, "The 2015 Rich List: The Highest Earning Hedge Fund Managers of the Past Year," *Institutional Investor's Alpha*, May 5, 2015, www.institutionalinvestorsalpha.com/Article/3450284/The-2015-Rich-List-The-Highest-Earning-Hedge-Fund-Managers-of-the-Past-Year.html.

22. Robin Greenwood and David Scharfstein, "The Growth of Finance," *Journal of Economic Perspectives* 27, no. 2 (Spring 2013): 3–28, doi: 10.1257/jep.27.2.3, http://pubs.aeaweb.org/doi/pdfplus/10.1257/jep.27.2.3.

23. Martin Neil Baily, "Stop Worrying. The Financial Sector Isn't Destroying the Economy," *Washington Post*, April 21, 2016, www.washingtonpost.com/news/in-theory/wp/2016/04/21/stop-worrying-the-finance-sector-isnt-destroying-the-economy/.

24. The lowest income households typically have only non-marketable implicit wealth in the form of expected future Social Security and Medicare benefits. Households just above that level sometimes have equity in their homes. Households that are still a little better off might have modest pension-account balances, whose trading is often restricted. Public policies can exacerbate rather than alleviate this inequality trend, by treating capital income more favorably than labor income. [*Tackling Economic Inequality, Boosting Opportunity: A Blueprint for Business*, (Arlington, VA: The Committee for Economic Development, April 2016), www.ced.org/pdf/CED-Inequality-Report.pdf.]

25. See, for example, Betsey Stevenson and Justin Wolfers, *Trust in Public Institutions over the Business Cycle*, Working Paper 2011-11 (San Francisco, CA: Federal Reserve Bank of San Francisco, March, 2011), www.frbsf.org/economic-research/files/wp11-11bk.pdf; "Sharp Drop in American Enthusiasm for Free Market, Poll Shows," Globescan, April 6, 2011, www.globescan.com/news-and-analysis/press-releases/press-releases-2011/94-press-releases-2011/150-sharp-drop-in-american-enthusiasm-for-free-market-poll-shows.html; and Max Ehrenfreund, "A Majority of Millennials Now Reject Capitalism, Survey Shows," *Wonkblog*, Washington Post, April 26, 2016, www.washingtonpost.com/news/wonk/wp/2016/04/26/a-majority-of-millennials-now-reject-capitalism-poll-shows/.

26. Nearly two out of three Americans believe income and wealth "should be more evenly distributed," Gallup research has consistently found. See, Frank Newport, "Americans Continue to Say U.S. Wealth Distribution is Unfair," Gallup, May 4, 2015, www.gallup.com/poll/182987/americans-continue-say-wealth-distribution-unfair.aspx.

27. Hannah Fingerhut, "Most Americans Say U.S. Economic System Is Unfair, But High Income Republicans Disagree," *Fact Tank*, Pew Research Center, February 10, 2016, www.pewresearch.org/fact-tank/2016/02/10/most-americans-say-u-s-economic-system-is-unfair-but-high-income-republicans-disagree/; *Pervasive Gloom About the World Economy*, Global Attitudes Project (Washington, D.C.: Pew Research Center, July 12, 2012), www.pewglobal.org/2012/07/12/pervasive-gloom-about-the-world-economy/; Andrew Ross Sorkin and Megan Thee-Brenan, "Many Feel the American Dream Is Out of Reach, Poll Shows," *DealBook*, New York Times, December 10, 2014, http://dealbook.nytimes.com/2014/12/10/many-feel-the-american-dream-is-out-of-reach-poll-shows/?_r=0.

28. See "The Party Winds Down," *The Economist*, May 7, 2016, www.economist.com/news/international/21698239-across-world-politically-connected-tycoons-are-feeling-squeeze-party-winds. *The Economist* maintains an annual "Crony Capitalism Index," measuring the number of crony sectors in an economy prone to public-private coziness. Nations are ranked relative to each other, based on how much of the economy is characterized by coziness. The United States ranked 16th in the magazine's 2016 index, behind Russia, Mexico, China, Brazil, and Britain, among other nations.

29. Government also subsidizes "public goods." Economists commonly argue that basic research and development must be subsidized, or even undertaken directly or indirectly by government, if the nation is to invest enough in vital new ideas. This is an example of a "public good," where the benefits of production or consumption "spill over" to the public at large, such that "free riders" can enjoy the benefit without paying. National defense is another clear example of a public good. A "spillover" could be negative, as well: a factory that generates dangerous by-products might cheaply dispose of them by dumping them in an adjacent river, to the detriment of society.

30. Matthew Mitchell, *The Pathology of Privilege: The Economic Consequences of Government Favoritism* (Arlington, VA: Mercatus Center at George Washington University, July 9,

31. John Beghin and Amani Elobeid, *The Impact of the U.S. Sugar Program Redux*, Working Paper 13-WP 538 (Ames, IA: Center for Agricultural and Rural Development at Iowa State University, May, 2013), http://lib.dr.iastate.edu/

cgi/viewcontent.cgi?article=1557&context=card_workingpapers;   Cameron
James Stokes, "Artificial Sweetness: A Survey of the Harmful Effects Caused
by the U.S. Sugar Program and Possibilities for Reform," *Georgetown Journal
of Law & Public Policy*, 10, no. 2 (Summer 2012): 589–618, doi: 10.2139/
ssrn.2205491. Cites an estimate from the National Confectioners Association
of 112,000 jobs lost in sugar-using industries between 1997 and 2009.

32. Timothy P. Carney, "Export-Import Bank 101: The 'it makes a profit' Argument,"
Washington Examiner, July 29, 2014, http://www.washingtonexaminer.com/
export-import-bank-101-the-it-makes-a-profit-argument/article/2551414.

33. Chris Bury, "Is This 1917 Law Suffocating Puerto Rico's Economy?," *News-
hour*, PBS, August 13, 2015, www.pbs.org/newshour/making-sense/jones-act-
holding-puerto-rico-back-debt-crisis/; Brian Slattery, Bryan Riley, and Nicolas
Loris, "Sink the Jones Act: Restoring America's Competitive Advantage in
Maritime-Related Industries," Backgrounder 2886, Heritage Foundation,
May 22, 2014, www.heritage.org/research/reports/2014/05/sink-the-jones-
act-restoring-americas-competitive-advantage-in-maritime-related-industries.

34. Martin S. Feldstein, Chair of the Council of Economic Advisers under President Ronald Reagan, defines "tax expenditures" as "those features of the tax
code that are a substitute for direct government spending." See Martin S.
Feldstein, "A Simple Route to Major Deficit Reduction," *Wall Street Journal*, February 20, 2013, www.wsj.com/articles/SB10001424127887324880
50457829692027892167676; and Martin S. Feldstein, "Raise Taxes, but Not
Tax Rates," *New York Times*, May 5, 2011, www.nytimes.com/2011/05/05/
opinion/05feldstein.html.

35. "Table 14.3—Total Government Expenditures as Percentages of GDP: 1948-
2015," Historical Tables, Budget of the United States Government, Fiscal
Year 2017, U.S. Office of Management and Budget, 2016, accessed September 2016, www.whitehouse.gov/omb/budget/Historicals.

36. Edmund Phelps, *Mass Flourishing: How Grassroots Innovation Created Jobs,
Challenge, and Change* (Princeton, NJ: Princeton University Press, 2013).
"Significant" here is defined in Executive Order 12866, issued September 30,
1993, which was intended to streamline the regulatory process.

37. Office of Management and Budget, *2014 Report to Congress on the Benefits and
Costs of Federal Regulations and Unfunded Mandates on State, Local, and Tribal
Entities* (Washington, D.C.: Office of Information and Regulatory Affairs,
Executive Office of the President of the United States, 2014), www.whitehouse
.gov/sites/default/files/omb/inforeg/2014_cb/2014-cost-benefit-report.pdf;
Christopher Demuth, "The Regulatory State," *National Affairs* 12 (Summer

2012),   www.nationalaffairs.com/publications/detail/the-regulatory-state makes the important point that the modern regulatory state is a bipartisan enterprise. He argues that during the half century before President Obama's election, the greatest growth in regulation came under Presidents Richard Nixon and George W. Bush, and that the latter set the stage for many of the subsequent Obama Administration regulatory initiatives.

38. Expressed as a percentage of GDP, some historical elections—in the economic crises of 1896 and 1932, and during the Vietnam War in 1968—have elicited extraordinary levels of campaign spending. Matthew O'Brien, "The Most Expensive Election Ever: . . . 1896?," *The Atlantic*, November 6, 2012, www .theatlantic.com/business/archive/2012/11/the-most-expensive-election-ever-1896/264649/. However, there has been a consistent upward trend even using this metric since 1996 (when spending was only slightly below 1992), and over those 16 years (five presidential election cycles inclusive), spending as a percentage of GDP has about tripled, and in 2012 was not far short of the post-World War II peak at the height of the Vietnam engagement in 1968. Measured in constant dollars rather than as a percentage of GDP, campaign spending has increased even more markedly.

39. Scott Blackburn, "Dire Predictions about Citizens United Prove False," *Washington Times*, January 29, 2015, www.washingtontimes.com/news/2015/ jan/29/scott-blackburn-dire-predictions-about-citizens-un/.

40. Luigi Zingales, *A Capitalism for the People: Recapturing the Lost Genius of American Prosperity* (Philadelphia: Basic Books, 2012).

41. Another form of public-private "deal" is the expansive use of patents and copyrights to protect an existing enterprise from fair competition, or alternatively to poach on the returns to true innovation with ambitious claims of intellectual property rights. Edmund Phelps notes that parallel to the increase in regulation there has been an explosion in patent and copyright protection that has stifled both innovation and competition. Phelps contends that in the high-tech industry there is such a thicket of patents in force that a creator of a new method might well require as many lawyers as engineers to move forward with his idea.

42. See John Figueiredo and Brian Richter, "Advancing the Empirical Research on Lobbying," *Annual Review of Political Science* 17 (May 2014): 163–185, doi: 10.1146/annurev-polisci-100711-135308, www.annualreviews.org/doi/ abs/10.1146/annurev-polisci-100711-135308?journalCode=polisci.

43. However, lobbying may be "defensive" rather than "offensive." That is, rather than pursuing preferential deals, firms may need to explain market conditions

to policymakers or regulators to avoid bad public policy, or to protect themselves from ideologically or competitively driven challenges from government or from other private entities.

44. Lee Drutman, "Lobbying and Declining Corporate Tax Burdens," Blog, Sunlight Foundation, March 27, 2013, https://sunlightfoundation.com/blog/2013/03/27/corporate-taxes/.

45. Similarly, Richter, Samphantharak, and Timmons found in their 2008 study on "Lobbying and Taxes" that firms that spend more on lobbying in a given year pay lower effective tax rates in the next year. According to their study, increasing registered lobbying expenditures by 1 percent appears to lower effective tax rates by somewhere in the range of 0.5 to 1.6 percentage points for the average firm that lobbies. Brian Kelleher Richter, Krislert Samphantharak, and Jeffrey F. Timmons, "Lobbying and Taxes," *American Journal of Political Science* 10, no. 4 (October 22, 2008): 893-909, doi: 10.2139/ssrn.1082146.

46. Richard L. Hall and Alan V. Deardorff, "Lobbying as Legislative Subsidy," *American Political Science Review* 10, no. 1 (February 2006).

47. Lawrence Lessig, *Republic, Lost: How Money Corrupts Congress—and a Plan to Stop It* (New York: Twelve, 2011).

48. Supreme Court of the United States, *McConnell, United States Senator, et al. v. Federal Election Commission et al.* (December 10, 2003), 14, footnote 13.

49. Adam Smith, *An Inquiry into the Nature and Causes of the Wealth of Nations* (Chicago: University of Chicago Press, 1976), Book 1, Chapter 10, 144.

50. Mancur Olson, *The Rise and Decline of Nations: Economic Growth, Stagflation, and Social Rigidities* (New Haven, CT: Yale University Press, 1982), 69.

51. Bo Cutter, Robert Litan, and Dane Stangler, *The Good Economy* (Roosevelt Institute and Kauffman Foundation, 2016), http://rooseveltinstitute.org/wp-content/uploads/2016/02/Good-Economy-Feb-29-2016.pdf.

52. Ibid.

53. Raj M. Desai and Anders Olofsgard, "The Cost of Political Influence: Firm Level Evidence from Developing Countries," *Quarterly Journal of Political Science* 6, no 2 (2011): 137–178. Of course, drawing cross-country lessons about crony activity is problematic, because crony behavior is highly situational. But this study is a useful example of the point we raise, not a data comparison.

54. Sorkin, Andrew Ross and Megan Thee-Brenan. "Many Feel American Dream Is Out of Reach, Poll Shows." Op.cit.

55. Luigi Zingales, for instance: See, *A Capitalism for the People*.

56. We use the term "shareholder-only model" throughout this chapter to refer to the theory that businesses are only responsible for maximizing their *owners'* value, although we are aware that only corporations have shareholders.

Nevertheless we use "shareholder-only model" since it is common in writing on corporate governance. However, the idea, and the multi-stakeholder model we advocate in its place, apply to both publicly and privately held companies.

57. Larry D. Thompson, "The Responsible Corporation: Its Historical Roots and Continuing Promise," *Notre Dame Journal of Law, Ethics & Public Policy* 29, no. 1 (2015): 199–230.

58. David H. Langstaff, "The Purpose of the Firm" (Keynote Address, Brookings Institution, December 13, 2011), https://assets.aspeninstitute.org/content/uploads/files/content/upload/Brookings%20Institute-Purpose%20of%20the%20Firm%20Speech-Dec%202011-FINAL.pdf.

59. Thompson, Larry D. "The Responsible Corporation." op.cit., takes the history back to the Roman Empire.

60. Milton Friedman, *Capitalism and Freedom* (Chicago: University of Chicago Press, 1962), 133; see also Eugene F. Fama and Michael C. Jensen, "Separation of Ownership and Control," *Journal of Law and Economics* 26 (June 1983): 301–326.

61. Marshall E. Blume and Donald B. Keim, *Institutional Investors and Stock Market Liquidity: Trends and Relationships* (The Wharton School, University of Pennsylvania, August 21, 2012), doi: 10.2139/ssrn.2147757; U.S. Securities and Exchange Commissioner, Luis A. Aguilar, "Institutional Investors: Power and Responsibility" (Speech, Center for the Economic Analysis of Risk, Georgia State University, April 19 2013), www.sec.gov/News/Speech/Detail/Speech/1365171515808; and National Investors Relations Institute, 2003 data point on top 1000 U.S. Corporations.

62. Stephen Davis, Jon Lukomnik, and David Pitt-Watson, *The New Capitalists: How Citizen Investors Are Reshaping the Corporate Agenda* (Boston: Harvard Business School Press, 2006), 50. In effect, these funds "internalize externalities:" they absorb both sides of the actions of one firm that fall upon another firm.

63. *2012 Report on Sustainable and Responsible Investing Trends in the United States* (Washington, D.C.: The Forum for Sustainable and Responsible Investment, 2012).

64. *Global Insights on ESG in Alternative Investing* (Mercer and LGT Capital Partners, March 2015), www.lgtcp.com/shared/.content/publikationen/$news_attachment/150210-ESG_Mercer_LGT.PDF.

65. Edelman Trust Barometer summaries are available on the company's website, www.edelman.com. See, particularly, the 2014 survey, in which the firm drilled down with survey respondents on some of these issues. "2014 Edelman Trust Barometer," Video, Edelman, accessed September 2016, www.edelman.com/insights/intellectual-property/2014-edelman-trust-barometer/.

66. See, for instance, the *Redefining Business Success in a Changing World: CEO Survey*, 19th Annual Global CEO Survey (PWC, January 2016), www.pwc.com/gx/en/ceo-survey/2016/landing-page/pwc-19th-annual-global-ceo-survey.pdf. PWC surveyed 1,400 executives in 86 countries, but when filtering the data to look at solely the responses of U.S. CEO's, nearly 70 percent of U.S. respondents agree.

67. See Chapter 6 on fiscal health.

68. The survey was conducted by McKinsey & Company and the Canadian Pension Plan Investment Board. See Dominic Barton and Mark Wiseman, "Focusing Capital on the Long Term," *Harvard Business Review* (January–February 2014), https://hbr.org/2014/01/focusing-capital-on-the-long-term.

69. John R. Graham, Campbell R. Harvey, and Shivaram Rajgopal, "Value Destruction and Financial Reporting Decisions," *Financial Analysts Journal* 62, no. 6 (November/December 2006): 27–39, doi: 10.2469/faj.v62.n6.4351.

70. *Measuring Productivity: Measurement of Aggregate and Industry-Level Productivity Growth*, OECD Manual (Paris, France: OECD Publications, 2001), 12–18, www.oecd.org/std/productivity-stats/2352458.pdf; Shawn Sprague, "What Can Labor Productivity Tell Us about the U.S. Economy?," *Beyond the Numbers*, BLS 3, no. 12, (May 2014), www.bls.gov/opub/btn/volume-3/what-can-labor-productivity-tell-us-about-the-us-economy.htm.

71. John R. Graham, Campbell R. Harvey, and Shiva Rajgopal, "The Economic Implications of Corporate Financial Reporting," *Journal of Accounting and Economics* 40 (Dec. 2005): 3–73.

72. John Asker, Joan Farre-Mensa, and Alexander Ljungqvist. "Corporate Investment and Stock Market Listing: A Puzzle?," *Review of Financial Studies* 28, no. 2 (February 2015): 342–390, doi: 10.2139/ssrn.1603484.

73. Michael J. Mauboussin, "Long-Term Investing in a Short-Term World: How Psychology and Incentives Shape the Investment Industry," Legg Mason Capital Management, May 18, 2006, 3, www.aberdeeninvestment.com/wp-content/uploads/2009/11/Long-Term_Investing_Short-Term_World-JBT-Marks.pdf; John C. Bogle, *The Battle for the Soul of Capitalism* (New Haven, CT: Yale University Press, 2005), 158.

74. World Federation of Exchanges, www.world-exchanges.org/home/; Dominic Barton and Mark Wiseman, "Focusing Capital on the Long Term," (Address, Institute of Corporate Directors, May 22, 2013), www.cppib.com/content/dam/cppib/common/en/PDF/Address_to_the_ICD_Focusing_Capital_on_the_Long_Term_May_22_2013_.pdf.

75. Theoreticians have mixed opinions about whether short-termism can even exist. Some hold to an "efficient market hypothesis," which holds that prices

of shares are indeed the best estimates of real value due to the efficient pricing of the stock market. Many others have shown that the violation of certain theoretical assumptions, such as the existence of momentum trading, makes short-termism not just possible but likely.

76. Yvan Allaire, "Does Hedge Fund 'Activism' Create Long Term Shareholder Value?" (Presentation, Annual Meeting of the Center for Corporate Governance, The Conference Board, November 14, 2014).

77. Donna Dabney, Melissa Aguilar, Gad Levanon, and Alexander Parkinson, *Is Short-term Behavior Jeopardizing the Future Prosperity of Business?*, Report R-1593-15 (New York: The Conference Board, 2015), www.conference-board. org/pdfdownload.cfm?masterProductID=9954., using data from Activist Insight, retrieved August 15, 2015.

78. Barton and Wiseman, op cit.

79. Mauboussin. "Long-Term Investing in a Short-Term World." 4.

80. Eduard Gracia, "Corporate Short-term Thinking and the Winner Take all Market," *B>Quest*, Richards College of Business, University of West Georgia, www.westga.edu/~bquest/2004/thinking.htm; Rachel Feintzeig, "Study: CEO Tenure on the Rise," *Wall Street Journal*, April 9, 2014, http://blogs.wsj. com/atwork/2014/04/09/study-ceo-tenure-on-the-rise/.

81. Moren Levesque, Phillip Phan, Steven Raymar, and Maya Waisman, "Are CEOs Myopic? A Dynamic Model of the Ongoing Debate," *Advances in Financial Economics* 17, (2014): 125–151, doi: 10.1108/S1569-373220140000017004; John Willman, "Finance Chiefs Bemoan Ceo Optimism," *Financial Times*, March 8, 2007, www.ft.com/cms/s/0/643d112e-cd1a-11db-a938-000b5df10621.html?ft_site=falcon&desktop=true#axzz4LfovGF5l.

82. This discussion relies on Michael J. Mauboussin and Alfred Rappaport, "Reclaiming the Idea of Shareholder Value," *Harvard Business Review*, July 1, 2016, https://hbr.org/2016/07/reclaiming-the-idea-of-shareholder-value. They refer to the firm's objectives as a "governing objective."

83. The CED has long advocated a pragmatic model for reforming the system used to determine executive pay in many U.S. corporations. We believe that framework remains a sound approach for reform. See *Private Enterprise, Public Trust: The State of Corporate America After Sarbanes-Oxley* (Washington, D.C.: Committee for Economic Development, March 21, 2006), 24–26, www.ced.org/reports/single/private-enterprise-public-trust-the-state-of-corporate-america-after-s.

84. Ben W. Heineman, Jr., *High Performance with High Integrity* (Boston: Harvard Business School Press, 2008), 154.

85. Finally, directors, too, should be required to hold the company's shares. *Built*

to Last: Focusing Corporations on Long-Term Performance (Washington, D.C.: Committee for Economic Development, 2007), www.ced.org/pdf/Built-to-Last.pdf. It should be noted that this recommendation is controversial—even among some trustees who oversaw the publication of CED's 2007 report.

86. Dominic Barton and Mark Wiseman, "Focusing Capital on the Long Term," *Harvard Business Review* (January–February 2014), https://hbr.org/2014/01/focusing-capital-on-the-long-term.

87. Dominic Barton and Mark Wiseman, "Where Boards Fall Short," *Harvard Business Review* (January–February 2015), https://hbr.org/2015/01/where-boards-fall-short.

88. *The College and Career Readiness of U.S. High School Graduates* (Washington, D.C.: Achieve, March 14, 2016), www.achieve.org/state-profiles.

89. Lynn A. Karoly and Anamarie Auger, *Informing Investments in Preschool Quality and Access in Cincinnati: Evidence of Impacts and Economic Returns from National, State, and Local Preschool Programs* (Santa Monica, CA: RAND Corporation, 2016), www.rand.org/pubs/research_reports/RR1461.html.

90. *Unfinished Business: Continued Investment in Child Care and Early Education Is Critical to Business and America's Future* (Washington, D.C.: Committee for Economic Development, 2012), www.ced.org/pdf/Unfinished-Business.pdf.

91. Ibid.

92. W. Steven Barnett, Megan E. Carolan, James H. Squires, Kirsty Clarke Brown, and Michelle Horowitz, *The State of Preschool 2014: State Preschool Yearbook* (New Brunswick, NJ: National Institute for Early Education Research, 2014), 6–7, http://nieer.org/sites/nieer/files/Yearbook2014_full2_0.pdf.

93. Grover J. (Russ) Whitehurst and Ellie Klein, "Do We Already Have Universal Preschool?," *Evidence Speaks Reports* 1, no. 1 (September 17, 2015): 1, www.brookings.edu/wp-content/uploads/2016/06/Evidence-Speaks-Report-vol1.pdf.

94. This is one of many examples in which our inability to come to grips with our fiscal challenges is resulting in the crowding out of public investment in much needed areas.

95. Claudia Goldin and Lawrence F. Katz, *The Race Between Education and Technology* (Cambridge, MA: Belknap Press, 2008).

96. These percentages are imputed from data for 2012 and the fall of 2013, since it is difficult to obtain comparable data for the numbers of public, private, and homeschool students for a single year. An estimated 3.4% of K12 students were homeschooled in 2012. Assuming that the same percentage of students (3.4%) were homeschooled in 2013 and using fall 2013 enrollment figures for public and private K12 schools implies that approximately 87.2% of K12

students were enrolled in public schools and approximately 9.4% were enrolled in private schools. "Table 206.10.: Number and percentage of homeschooled students ages 5 through 17 with a grade equivalent of kindergarten through 12th grade, by selected child, parent, and household characteristics: 2003, 2007, and 2012," *Digest of Education Statistics: 2014*, National Center for Education Statistics, Institute of Education Statistics, 2014, https://nces.ed.gov/programs/digest/d14/tables/dt14_206.10.asp; "Table 203.20.: Enrollment in public elementary and secondary schools, by region, state, and jurisdiction: Selected years, fall 1990 through fall 2025," *Digest of Education Statistics: 2015*, National Center for Education Statistics, Institute of Education Statistics, 2015, http://nces.ed.gov/programs/digest/d15/tables/dt15_203.20.asp?current=yes; and "Table 205.20.: Enrollment and percentage distribution of students enrolled in private elementary and secondary schools, by school orientation and grade level: Selected years, fall 1995 through fall 2013," *Digest of Education Statistics: 2015*, National Center for Education Statistics, Institute of Education Statistics, 2015, http://nces.ed.gov/programs/digest/d15/tables/dt15_205.20.asp?current=yes.

97. "Public High School Graduation Rates," National Center for Education Statistics, May 2015, https://nces.ed.gov/programs/coe/pdf/coe_coi.pdf.

98. Many other studies, including ones conducted by individual states, reflect similar findings. See also *Beyond the Rhetoric: Improving College Readiness Through Coherent State Policy* (National Center for Public Policy and Higher Education and the Southern Regional Board, June 2010), www.highereducation.org/reports/college_readiness/CollegeReadiness.pdf.

99. Even this three-part model is oversimplified. In addition to the three elements listed above, a school's *culture and climate* affect both teachers and students in a school. The quality of *school leadership*, in turn, shapes a school's culture and climate, as well as other decisions that affect student learning. Finally, a school's *resources*, including most notably funding, affect all other aspects of learning. All these elements can be understood as providing the context in which learning occurs. For this piece, we have chosen to simplify by focusing on the "learning triad" of students, teachers, and what is taught because in the "magic" moment that learning occurs these three elements are most immediate and present, but this is not to deny the importance of the other, contextual elements.

100. Lynn A. Karoly and Anamarie Auger, "Informing Investments in Preschool Quality and Access in Cincinnati," op.cit.

101. Most school districts use a "single salary schedule" to determine teacher pay. This approach ignores teacher performance as a criterion for compensation. By not allowing for differential pay rates for certain subjects (e.g., math and

science) or for serving at hard-to-staff schools, single salary schedules contribute to persistent teacher shortages in these subjects and schools. Single salary schedules also do not create incentives for professional development that increases teacher effectiveness in the classroom. Such salary schedules reward teachers primarily for years of service and advanced degrees rather than for performance or effectiveness.

102. For example, Virginia's "Standards of Learning" governs 12 subjects for K12 schools. Virginia's Standards of Learning for English, alone, are 45 pages long.

103. States also had to test high school students once before graduation in English language arts and mathematics. Students had to be tested in science at least once in elementary, middle, and high school, for a total of three times.

104. We know this because we can compare the percentage of students deemed "proficient" on the National Assessment of Educational Progress (NAEP) tests in reading or math to the percentage of students deemed proficient in these areas on the state test. In some states, for example, as many as 86% of 4th graders were deemed proficient in reading on the state test, compared to only 28% who scored "proficient" on the NAEP. NAEP is a nationally representative assessment of what U.S. students know and can do at various grade levels. Thus it serves as a useful way to compare how rigorous various state tests are. "Students Meeting State Proficiency Standards and Performing at or Above the NAEP *Proficient* Level: 2009," National Center for Education Statistics, Institute of Education Sciences, September 1, 2011, https://nces.ed.gov/nationsreportcard/studies/statemapping/2009_naep_state_table.aspx.

105. See *How Business Leaders Can Support College- and Career-Readiness: Staying the Course on Common Core* (Washington DC: Committee for Economic Development, September 2014), www.ced.org/pdf/White_Paper.pdf. For a summary history of the Common Core and its implementation, as well as recommendations for steps businesses can take to advance the college- and career-ready standards.

106. "Your financial aid calculator: Calculate your estimated net price direct from schools before you apply," College Abacus, accessed September 2016, https://collegeabacus.org/.

107. Anthony P. Carnevale, Ban Cheah, and Andrew R. Hanson, *The Economic Value of College Majors* (Washington, D.C.: Center on Education and the Workforce, McCourt School of Public Policy, Georgetown University, 2015), https://cew.georgetown.edu/wp-content/uploads/The-Economic-Value-of-College-Majors-Full-Report-web-FINAL.pdf.

108. Jonathan Rothwell and Siddharth Kulkarni, *Beyond College Rankings: A Value-Added Approach to Assessing Two- and Four-Year Schools* (Washington, D.C.:

Metropolitan Policy Program at Brookings, April 2015), www.brookings.edu/
wp-content/uploads/2015/04/BMPP_CollegeValueAdded.pdf.

109. *Falling Short? College Learning and Career Success* (Washington, D.C.:
Hart Research Associates, January 20, 2015), www.aacu.org/leap/public-
opinion-research/2015-survey-results.

110. Richard Arum and Josipa Roksa, *Academically Adrift: Limited Learning on College Campuses* (Chicago: University of Chicago Press, 2011).

111. Bruce Ackerman and Ian Ayres, *Voting with Dollars: A New Paradigm for
Campaign Finance* (New Haven, CT: Yale University Press, 2002); Lawrence
Lessig, *Republic Lost*, Twelve, 2011; Luigi Zingales, *A Capitalism for the Peo-
ple*, Basic Books, 2012.

112. Some states that elect judges use a commission for purposes of interim replace-
ments, or to evaluate candidates who stand for election or for retention.

113. For example, in the House, the two Congresses with the largest numbers
of "closed rules" (forestalling to at least some degree the offering of amendments by the minority) were the 113th (2013–2014), under the control of the
Republican Party, and the 110th (2007–2008), under the control of the Democratic Party. Majorities under both parties in the Senate have decried the fil-
ibuster; minorities under both parties have employed it. Both parties in the
Senate have demanded up-or-down votes for presidential nominees when a
president of their party was in office, and have forestalled votes under a president of the other party.

114. It is important to note that it is neither improper nor unfair for the nation to
carry debt. Nations pass both financial and nonfinancial legacies on to the
next generation. Many of the nonfinancial assets that we leave to succeeding
generations—such as our freedom—were purchased at a dear price, including
(but certainly not limited to) money. For that reason, many reasonable and
prudent people would not consider it out of line that current American generations leave some of the costs of those nonfinancial assets, that is, a net financial public debt, to their successor generations.

115. "Table 7.1," Historical Tables, The Budget, Office of Management and Budget, www.whitehouse.gov/omb/budget/Historicals. The dollar amount of the
debt at the end of fiscal year 1946 is known with precision. The amount of the
GDP has been estimated from historical economic data, and is revised periodically; hence this historical number changes over time.

116. Note that many U.S. state and local governments also have serious budget
problems, sometimes partially hidden in the form of future state employee
pension liabilities. Such state and local government debt does not directly
add to that of the federal government. But realistically, the financial markets

easily could conclude that the federal government would find itself with no alternative to taking on some of that lower-level government debt. If the markets were to become skeptical about the safety of the federal government's own debt, the existing of state and local government debt problems can only exacerbate the risk. The economic impact of any state government crisis, indirectly raising federal spending and decreasing federal revenues, would only add to the potential market reaction. The ultimate economic impact of remedying state *and* federal budget crises would come out of the same consumer pocket, and so would be the same.

117. In fact, this is the argument the Committee for Economic Development accepted in the wake of the financial crisis. The CED concluded that extra spending by government would cascade into greater demand throughout the economy and generate employment; so long as unemployment remained high, budget deficits would not encourage inflation. This is what happened and it arguably arrested what could have been a more catastrophic downturn, or even another Great Depression.

118. Debt-to-GDP ran roughly 25 percent during the 1970s; rose to 50 percent by the early 1990s; fell back to less than 33 percent by 2001; and then shot up to 75 percent after the financial crisis.

119. See *The Budget and Economic Outlook: 2016 to 2026* (Washington, D.C.: Congressional Budget Office, January 2016), 131–135, www.cbo.gov/sites/ default/files/114th-congress-2015-2016/reports/51129-2016Outlook_OneCol-2 .pdf.; and Office of Management and Budget, *Analytical Perspectives: Budget of the U.S. Government, Fiscal Year 2017* (Washington, D.C.: U.S. Government Printing Office, 2016), 7–20, https://www.whitehouse.gov/sites/default/files/ omb/budget/fy2017/assets/spec.pdf., for estimates of the sensitivity of budget outcomes to changes in the assumed rate of growth.

120. For a more-detailed discussion of what could befall our debt-laden government and economy, see *This Way Down to a Debt Crisis* (Washington, D.C.: Committee for Economic Development, January 25, 2011), www.ced.org/ pdf/This-Way-Down.pdf.

121. Estimates vary. In 2014, the Congressional Research Service estimated that 13 years of war had cost $1.6 trillion for military operations in Afghanistan and Iraq, along with enhanced security of U.S. bases and embassies, veteran medical care, and aid to Iraq and Afghanistan. Earlier, in 2013, Harvard University researchers estimated war costs to run between $4–6 trillion, particularly when factoring in long-term care costs and benefits for veterans. (See Linda J. Bilmes, *The Financial Legacy of Iraq and Afghanistan: How Wartime Spending Decisions Will Constrain Future National Security Budgets*, Working Paper

RWP 13-006 (Cambridge, MA: Harvard Kennedy School, March 2013)). As of April 2015, The Watson Institute for International and Public Affairs, at Brown University, estimated the cost is $4.4 trillion, covering "direct Congressional war appropriations; war-related increases to the Pentagon base budget; veterans care and disability; increases in the homeland security budget; interest payments on direct war borrowing; foreign assistance spending; and estimated future obligations for veterans' care." (See "Cost of War: Economic Costs," Watson Institute for International and Public Affairs, Brown University, September 2016, http://watson.brown.edu/costsofwar/costs/economic.)

122. Compounding financial market concern about our excessive debt level in the near and medium term could well be the already elevated size of the Federal Reserve's balance sheet, plus restrictions on the Fed's role as a "lender of last resort." Hal S. Scott, "The Federal Reserve: The Weakest Lender of Last Resort Among its Peers," *International Finance* 18, no. 3 (November 2015): 321–342, http://onlinelibrary.wiley.com/doi/10.1111/infi.12075/abstract.

123. *Debt Limit: Market Response to Recent Impasses Underscores Need to Consider Alternative Approaches*, Report to the Congress, GAO-15-476 (Washington, D.C.: United States Government Accountability Office, July 2015), www.gao.gov/assets/680/671286.pdf.

124. The goal of the most recent revision of the Domenici-Rivlin plan was to set the debt-to-GDP ratio on a downward path to below 70 percent within 10 years, and below 60 percent within 30 years. The passage of time and subsequent changes in economic conditions would change the specific estimates but not the direction of the results of these policy steps.

125. *The 2016 Long-Term Budget Outlook* (Washington, D.C.: Congressional Budget Office, July 2016), www.cbo.gov/sites/default/files/114th-congress-2015-2016/reports/51580-LTBO-One-Col-2.pdf. The figures quoted in the text ignore Medicare offsetting receipts, which would not affect the conclusion.

126. Some might argue that the fault should be assigned to a shortfall of revenue. That argument could be made over a short period of time. But in the long run, Medicare costs are projected to grow faster than the GDP. Tax revenue cannot possibly keep pace with these costs

127. Note that choice among competing health care *plans*—during an annual open season, at comparative leisure—is not at all like choice among *procedures, providers,* and *hospitals* in "consumer directed health plans"—in effect patients trying to be their own doctors when they are sick and possibly in urgent need of care. The latter type of choice will be right for some beneficiaries, but certainly not for all.

128. As of 1997, the option to receive Medicare coverage through private plans was named "Medicare+Choice." The Medicare Modernization Act of 2003

(which most notably introduced Medicare prescription drug coverage) gave the program its current name.

129. An auction at the second-lowest bid—often referred to as a "Vickrey Auction," named after William Vickrey, the economist who won a Nobel Prize for its theoretical discovery—also has the property that the winning bidder has an incentive to provide a bid that more accurately and honestly reflects his valuation of the item at auction. William Vickrey, "Counterspeculation, Auctions, and Competitive Sealed Tenders," *Journal of Finance* 16, no. 1 (March 1961): 8-37.

130. *Modernizing Medicare* (Arlington, VA: Committee for Economic Development, forthcoming, October 2016).

131. Policy Statement on Fiscal Health (Arlington, VA: Committee for Economic Development, forthcoming, November 2016).

132. Public-private partnerships work well in financing infrastructure projects when the underlying project makes economic sense; the process to select a private partner is sound; and the revenue stream from the project is sufficient to provide an appropriate return. *Bridging Global Infrastructure Gaps* (McKinsey Global Institute, June 2016), 19–22.

133. The 28% rate applies approximately to income above $51,000 for single filers and $102,000 for couples.

134. $500 for singles and heads of household.

135. The refundable earnings credit is equal to 17.5% of the first $20,000 of earnings.

136. According to Tax Policy Center projections, only 50% of tax units would be required to file tax returns, as opposed to 88% under the current tax system.

137. We specify that, to justify intervention, market failures should be "material" because the very mass of regulation imposes costs on the economy. At the end of 2015, 3,410 final rules were issued, and 2,342 rules were pending; and the *Federal Register* for that year totaled 80,260 pages, for the third-highest number in history. (Clyde Wayne Crews Jr., *Ten Thousand Commandments* (Washington, D.C.: Competitive Enterprise Institute, 2016), https://cei.org/sites/default/files/Wayne%20Crews%20-%20Ten%20Thousand%20Commandments%202016%20-%20May%204%202016.pdf. These numbers refer only to federal regulations, not to the additional amount of state and local government regulations.) This mass of regulatory activity might be manageable for a large firm with a single-purpose legal department, but could constitute a crushing administrative burden for the new and small businesses that are the source of much innovation and economic growth. Although a strong argument can be made in favor of a regulation whose benefits exceed

its costs, those costs should include a fair measure of the burden on economic activity of the totality of regulation.

138. Bruce Yandle, "Bootleggers and Baptists: The Education of a Regulatory Economist," *Regulation* 7, no. 3 (May/June 1983): 12; Adam Smith and Bruce Yandle, *Bootleggers and Baptists: How Economic Forces and Moral Persuasion Interact to Shape Regulatory Politics* (Washington, D.C.: Cato Institute Press, 2014).

139. Frank Newport, "Little Appetite in U.S. for More Gov't Regulation of Business," Poll, Gallup, September 24, 2012, www.gallup.com/poll/157646/little-appetite-gov-regulation-business.aspx.

140. For example, Art Fraas and Alex Egorenkov, *A Retrospective Study of EPA's Rules Setting Best Available Technology Limits for Toxic Discharges to Water under the Clean Water Act*, Paper RFF DP 15-41 (Washington, D.C.: Resources for the Future Discussion, September 2015), www.rff.org/files/document/file/RFF-DP-15-41.pdf. Found little benefit from the BAT requirement. This study also confirmed our conclusion that more emphasis on data collection is needed to achieve high-quality retrospective analysis.

141. The recent Volkswagen diesel scandal has focused attention on efforts to manipulate standards of compliance with highly technical rules. Examples extend beyond auto emissions to the calculation of benchmark interest rates John Gapper, "Volkswagen's Deception Is a Warning to Every Company," *Financial Times*, September 23, 2015, www.ft.com/content/9e4a72a2-2f8c-11e5-91ac-a5e17d9b4cff.

142. Arnold Kling, "Why We Need Principles-Based Regulation," *The American*, May 22, 2012, www.aei.org/publication/why-we-need-principles-based-regulation/.

143. He notes, for instance, "the intentional dismissal of the cost of job displacement remains a real shortcoming of [federal regulatory] agency efforts to promote only those regulations where the benefits are worth their costs." Mercatus Center, March 2013. See also Cary Coglianese, Adam M. Finkel, and Christopher Carrigan, ed., *Does Regulation Kill Jobs?* (Philadelphia: University of Pennsylvania Press, 2013).

144. For an archetypical example, weighing the costs and benefits of regulations whose benefits include saving human lives require valuing life itself. A classic reference is Thomas Schelling, "The Life You Save May Be Your Own," in *Problems in Public Expenditure Analysis*, ed. Samuel B. Chase (Washington, D.C.: Brookings Institution, 1968).

145. It is also true that regulatory policies are not imposed in a vacuum, so without the more detailed data it's very difficult to attribute changes in business or

household behavior as due entirely to the regulatory policy. Micro-level data are needed to control for other factors affecting decisions and outcomes.

146. Joseph S. Shapiro and Reed Walker, *Why Is Pollution from U.S. Manufacturing Declining? The Roles of Trade, Regulation, and Preferences*, NBER Working Paper No. 20879 (Cambridge, MA: National Bureau of Economic Research, January 2015), http://www.nber.org/papers/w20879.

147. See for instance, Executive order 12866 by Bill Clinton, in 1993, OMB Circular A-4 (George W. Bush Administration), 2003, and Executive Orders 13563, 13579, and 13610, by Barak Obama, in 2011 and 2012. As of this writing, several legislative proposals under consideration are aimed at improving analysis for decision-making before regulations are issued and institutionalizing retrospective review after they are put into place. These include: S.1818, S.1820, and S.1607.

148. See Susan Dudley, "A Review of Regulatory Reform Proposals" (Testimony, U.S. Senate Committee on Homeland Security and Governmental Affairs, September 16, 2015), www.hsgac.senate.gov/hearings/a-review-of-regulatory-reform-proposals.

149. *Reexamining Regulations: Agencies Often Made Regulatory Changes, but Could Strengthen Linkages to Performance Goals*, GA0-14-268 (Washington, D.C.: United States Government Accountability Office, April 2014), http://www.gao.gov/assets/670/662517.pdf.

150. Alternatively, Congress could establish a separate organization to do this, or the function could be located in the Congressional Budget Office or the Government Accountability Office. However, OIRA already is the major centralized resource of regulatory expertise in Washington, and is charged with the final approval of new regulations. OIRA (a part of the Office of Management and Budget) has a reputation of impartial expertise, which would be essential for the function of ex-post regulatory review (as it is for regulatory approval as well).

151. *The Governance of Regulators: OECD Best Practice Principles for Regulatory Policy* (Paris, France: OECD Publishing, 2014), doi: 10.1787/9789264209015-en, www.oecd.org/gov/regulatory-policy/governance-of-regulators.htm.

152. Jonathan Weisman, "U.S. Declares Bank and Auto Bailouts Over, and Profitable," *New York Times*, December 19, 2014, www.nytimes.com/2014/12/20/business/us-signals-end-of-bailouts-of-automakers-and-wall-street.html.

153. Hal S. Scott, *Connectedness and Contagion: Protecting the Financial System from Panics* (Cambridge, MA: MIT Press, 2016). A more esoteric issue is the emergence and growth of outstanding non-bank short-term debt. Some argue that excessive subprime lending and leverage throughout the financial system would not have been possible without the growing creation of cash-equivalent

(and hence subject to runs) short-term debt created outside the banking system. Others believe that there were other far more commonplace sources of short-term credit that actually could play the same role. A radical approach to head off this potential problem would be simply to ban non-bank financial institutions from issuing liabilities with a maturity of one year or less. This would constitute what some might call an end to shadow banking. See Morgan Ricks, *The Money Problem: Rethinking Financial Regulation* (Chicago: University of Chicago Press, 2016).

154. "Trade growth to remain subdued in 2016 as uncertainties weigh on global demand," World Trade Organization, April 7, 2016, www.wto.org/english/news_e/pres16_e/pr768_e.htm.

155. Council of Economic Advisors, *The Economic Benefits of U.S. Trade* (Washington, D.C.: Executive Office of the President of the United States, May, 2015), www.whitehouse.gov/sites/default/files/docs/cea_trade_report_final_non-embargoed_v2.pdf.

156. Arvind Subramanian and Martin Kessler, *The Hyperglobalization of Trade and Its Future,* Working Paper WP 13-6 (Washington, D.C.: Peterson Institute for International Economics, July 2013), https://piie.com/sites/default/files/publications/wp/wp13-6.pdf.

157. Authors' calculations. World Bank, foreign direct investment. "Foreign direct investment, net inflows (BoP, current US$)," The World Bank, accessed September 2016, http://data.worldbank.org/indicator/BX.KLT.DINV.CD.WD; and "GDP (current US$)," The World Bank, accessed September 2016, http://data.worldbank.org/indicator/NY.GDP.MKTP.CD; and "Gross Domestic Product (GDP)," Bureau of Economic Analysis, U.S. Department of Commerce, http://www.bea.gov/national/index.htm#gdp.

158. Council of Economic Advisors, *The Economic Benefits of U.S. Trade* (Washington, D.C.: Executive Office of the President of the United States, May, 2015), www.whitehouse.gov/sites/default/files/docs/cea_trade_report_final_non-embargoed_v2.pdf.

159. "KOF index of globalization," KOF Swiss Economic Institute, accessed September 2016, http://globalization.kof.ethz.ch/. Also see Axel Dreher, "Does Globalization Affect Growth? Evidence from a New Index of Globalization," *Applied Economics* 38, no 10 (2006): 1091–1110, doi: 10.1080/00036840500392078.

160. Trade Adjustment Assistance (TAA) was created in 1962 and expanded during the 1990s (and as part of the negotiations for the NAFTA agreement). It was supported by both Republican and Democratic administrations. See *Making Trade Work: Straight Talk on Jobs, Trade, and Adjustment* (Washington,

D.C.: Committee for Economic Development, March 2005), www.ced
.org/pdf/Making-Trade-Work.pdf.

161. See Giovanni Peri, *The Effect of Immigration on Productivity: Evidence from US States*, Working Paper 15507 (Cambridge, MA: National Bureau of Economic Research, November 2009), doi: 10.3386/w15507, www.nber.org/papers/w15507.pdf; Gianmarco I. P. Ottaviano, Giovanni Peri, and Greg C. Wright, "Immigration, Offshoring, and American Jobs," *American Economic Review* 103, no. 5 (August, 2013), 1925–59, doi: 10.3386/w16439; and *Modern Immigration Wave Brings 59 Million to U.S., Driving Population Growth and Change Through 2065: Views of Immigration's Impact on U.S. Society Mixed* (Washington, D.C.: Pew Research Center, September 28, 2015), www.pewhispanic.org/files/2015/09/2015-09-28_modern-immigration-wave_REPORT.pdf.

162. *More Mexicans Leaving Than Coming to the U.S.: Net Loss of 140,000 from 2009 to 2014; Family Reunification Top Reason for Return* (Washington, D.C.: Pew Research Center, November 2015), www.pewhispanic.org/2015/11/19/more-mexicans-leaving-than-coming-to-the-u-s/. Apprehensions of illegal immigrants from Mexico have fallen almost consistently over the last decade—from 1.1 million in 2005, to 0.88 million in 2008 (at the height of the financial crisis), to 0.35 million in 2014 (the latest year for which data are available). Total apprehensions also generally declined, from 1.3 million in 2005, to 1.0 million in 2008, and to 0.68 million in 2014. The numbers of persons obtaining lawful permanent resident status was flat to down over the same period. The number of refugee arrivals increased slightly, but the numbers are small and their change is overwhelmed by the changes in other categories. Office of Immigration Statistics, *2014 Yearbook of Immigration Statistics* (Washington, D.C.: Department of Homeland Security, August 2016), especially Table 34, page 93. www.dhs.gov/sites/default/files/publications/ois_yb_2014.pdf.

163. *Modern Immigration Wave Brings 59 Million to U.S., Driving Population Growth and Change Through 2065* (Washington, D.C: Pew Research Center, September 28, 2015), 34-50, www.pewhispanic.org/files/2015/09/2015-09-28_modern-immigration-wave_REPORT.pdf; Francine D. Blau and Christopher Mackie, ed., *The Economic and Fiscal Consequences of Immigration* (Washington, D.C.: National Academies Press, 2016), 65–121, www.nap.edu/catalog/23550/the-economic-and-fiscal-consequences-of-immigration.

164. *Help Wanted: What Looming Labor Shortages Mean for Your Business* (New York: The Conference Board, April 2016), www.conference-board.org/publications/publicationdetail.cfm?publicationid=7191.

165. Martin Wolf, "Globalization in a Time of Transition," *Financial Times*, July 16, 2013, www.ft.com/content/9545cd9e-ed3c-11e2-ad6e-00144feabdc0.

INDEX

Federal Reserve, 136
Fee-for-service health care, 108, 110, 112, 156
Filibusters, 85, 179n113
Financial downturn of 2008, 3, 7–9, 29, 100
  causes of, 133–134, 136–137
Financial events affecting public debt, 100–101
Financial sector, 8, 24–25
  big banks in, 40, 136
  and economic inequality, 24–25
  government support of, 134–135, 137
  growth of, 25, 26
  international institutions in, 136
  lending practices of, 133–134, 136–137, 184–185n153
  and non-bank short-term debt, 184–185n153
  regulation and reform of, 13, 24, 133–138
Free enterprise, value of, 5–7
Friedman, Milton, 44

General Electric Ecomagination initiative, 55
Gift economy, 39
Global economy, 23–24, 25–26, 28
  adjustment policies in, 144–145, 160–161
  economic inequality in, 29, 140
  equality of opportunity in, 26, 138
  Export-Import Bank in, 33–34
  international coordination and cooperation in, 148–149, 162–163
  job-search assistance in, 145, 161
  knowledge-based, 25
  skills needed in, 23, 25, 139, 140, 141, 144–145, 161
  sustainable capitalism in, 139–150
  technological innovations in, 23–24, 140, 141
  trade in. See Trade, global
  wage insurance in, 145, 161
Government
  annual spending of, 35
  comparison of pro-business and pro-market policies, 42
  cronyism in, 29–42. See also Crony capitalism

defense spending of. See Defense spending
education funding of, 62–65, 74
ethics violations in, 81, 158
and financing of election campaigns. See Campaign financing
gridlock in, 2, 26
intervention in market failure, 31, 32
lobbying of. See Lobbying
loss of trust in, 2, 75
policy-making process in. See Policy-making process
private interests influencing, 30
and public debt. See Public debt
redistricting practices in, 77, 82–83, 158–159
regulations of. See Regulations
short-termism in deficit-spending by, 49–50
vital center of, 75, 77, 84–86
Government Accountability Office, 81, 127, 158
Graduation rate from high schools, 66
Great Depression, 3, 7, 17
Gross domestic product
  and defense spending, 113
  and global trade, 142, 143
  and Medicare spending, 106, 181n126
  and productivity, 21
  and public debt, 87, 90–91, 95–99, 106, 179n115, 180n118
  and total government spending, 35

Hagel, Chuck, 39
Hall, Keith, 126
Hall, Richard, 39
Health care, 12, 76, 155–156
  consumer choice in, 110–111, 155–156
  fee-for-service, 108, 110, 112, 156
  Medicare in. See Medicare
  tax exclusions on insurance for, 35, 117
High school education, 65–69, 70
Home loans, 133–134
Homeschooling, 176–177n96

IBM Smarter Planet platform, 55
Immigration policies, 93–94, 141
  in Canada, 148, 162